The Institute of African American Psychology

(IAAP)

"Using psychological science to create equal opportunities for achieving the American Dream."

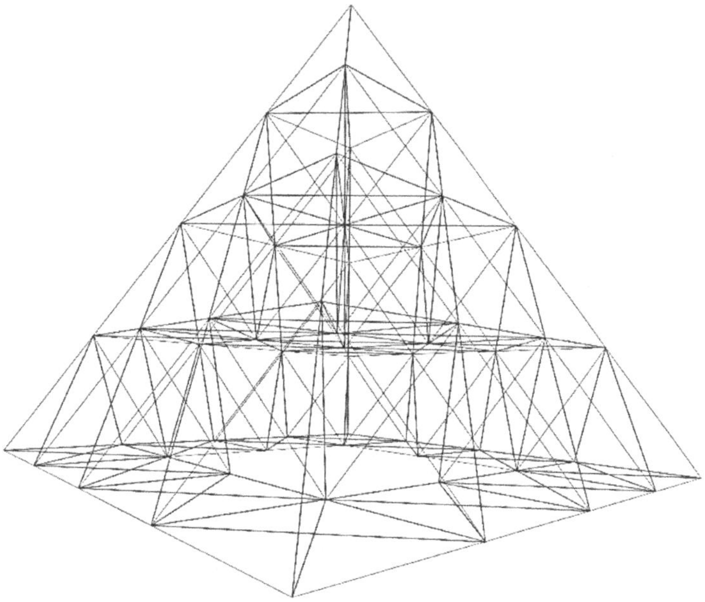

The Psychology of Racism

VOLUME I.

The Psychology of Racism

VOLUME I.

SECTION I.

MADE IN AMERICA: THE PSYCHOLOGICAL EVOLUTION OF THE BLACK MALE

SECTION II.

EXCUSE OR EXPLANATION: AN ANSWER TO THE CAUSE OF BLACK MALE UNDERACHIEVEMENT

SECTION III.

RECONDITIONING SOULS: THE ART AND SCIENCE OF COUNSELING BLACK MALES

Andre R. Fields, Ph.D.

IAAP Publishing

The Institute of African American Psychology

IAAP Publishing

FOR INFORMATION:

IAAP Publishing

PHONE: 616.323.8506

EMAIL: afields@theiaap.org

WEBSITE: www.theiaap.org

Special discounts on bulk quantities are available.

For information contact: www.theiaap.org

Cover Design: Piper Adonya
piperadonya.com

Printed in the United States of America

A catalog record of this book is available from the Library of Congress.

ISBN-13: 978-0692484548
ISBN-10: 069248454X

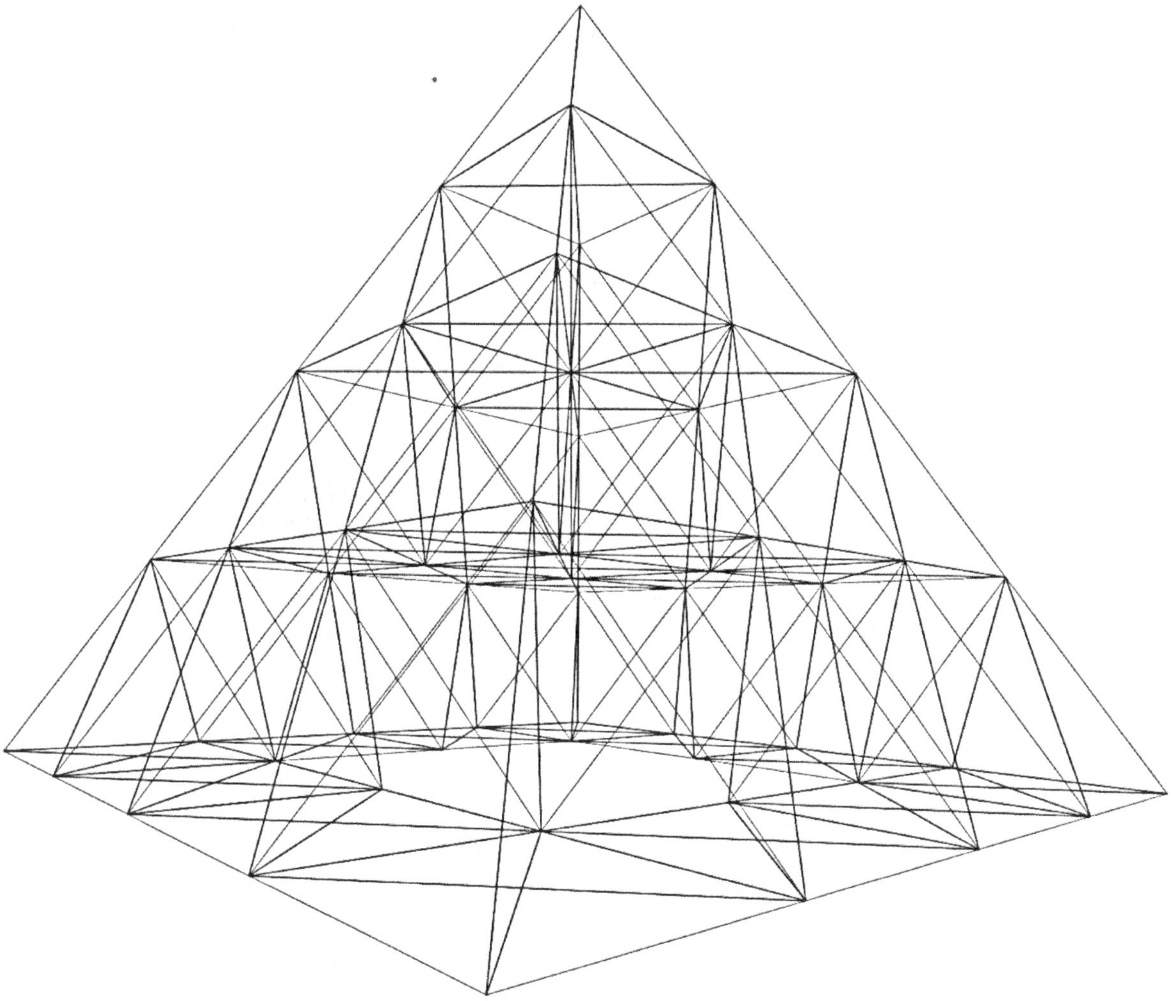

BOOK CONTENTS

The Psychology of Racism

Volume I

SECTION I.

MADE IN AMERICA: THE PSYCHOLOGICAL EVOLUTION OF THE BLACK MALE

SECTION II.

EXCUSE OR EXPLANATION: AN ANSWER TO THE CAUSE OF BLACK MALE UNDERACHIEVEMENT

SECTION III.

RECONDITIONING SOULS: THE ART AND SCIENCE OF COUNSELING BLACK MALES

"Once America includes all categories of its citizens, America will be able to truly serve as the measuring stick by which all societies, governments, and nations are measured as it relates to social morality and respect for humanity"

- *A.R.F.*

Andre R. Fields, Ph.D.

Founder and Director
The Institute of African American Psychology
(IAAP)

When you are talking about the Black male problem you are not talking about a recent issue or current affair. When you are talking about the Black male problem you are talking about a problem that has regenerated itself in every generation of American history. Even today, as we press deeper into the present millennium, the gap separating the social progress of Black males and other racial groups continues to increase. I believe that these statistical gaps are caused by psychological struggles, which are rooted in toxic social experiences encountered during the Black male's lifespan.

If you were to read through the pages of American history, you would find that racism and a lack of education have always been the two most debilitating and sabotaging barriers to the Black male's pursuit of the American Dream. It is my theoretical position that Race-Specific Underachievement Issues (education, underemployment, criminality, poverty, etc.) are related to Race-Specific Psychological Issues (hopelessness, low self-efficacy, decreased motivation, etc.), which are related to Race-Specific Social Experiences (racism, stigma, and discrimination).

Despite the generational travesty of Black males experiencing extreme social hardship, minimal research has been devoted to investigating the psychological experiences of this portion of the American population. As a result, there is now a collective deficit of psychological science related to improving the mental and emotional functioning of Black males. I have made improving the life outcomes of Black males my moral and professional responsibility. Thus, the strategic goal of this book is to equip Black males with the psychological resources necessary to overcome the societal factors that have traditionally complicated the psychological development and life outcomes of this portion of the American population.

It is my professional practice to utilize the science of psychology to develop curriculums, frameworks, and interventions that enhance and expand the capacity for institutions and organizations to effectively serve their Black male clientele. By systematically researching the psychological experiences of Black males, evidence-based treatment models can be created and eventually work to prevent and/or remedy the psychological impact of the racism, stigma, and discrimination.

In conclusion to this message, it is my ultimate purpose to enhance the mental, emotional, and behavioral functioning of the Black male population, so that collectively, they are more effective at overcoming the problematic social and cultural barriers they face on a daily basis. The current social epidemic of underachievement by Black males is a "national emergency". Beyond being a national emergency, this epidemic is truly an American tribulation that has to be brought to a final end. Despite its profoundly complicated nature this problem can be solved! This book was written with a spirit of belief and knowing. It was written with a deep knowing that Americans of all races are willing to invest their intelligence, empathy, time, and energy into bringing an end to the dark American travesty of Black male underachievement.

Andre Fields, Ph.D.

Every page of this book is dedicated to every boy, every man, and every mind that was ever wasted.

SECTION I.

Made in America: The Psychological Evolution of the Black Male

The Psychology of Racism 1.

Made in America: The Psychological Evolution of the Black Male

The American ~~Dream~~ Nightmare

One of America's most profound tragedies has been its transgenerational, racially-motivated, maltreatment of Black males. This relentless and systematic maltreatment has spanned well over 500 years. In comparison to every other social group (racial or ethnic), Black males have had their existence complicated to the greatest degree by America's racially-oppressive devices. During the past five centuries of America's short history, it has been shamefully documented that Black males of all generations, have been systematically denied the most fundamental and inalienable of all citizenry rights - *the right to a true and equal path to the American Dream.*

Even in today's 21st century, one of the bleakest realities confronting America is its continued reproduction of educationally underachieving and socially detached Black males. America's laissez-faire attitude and unhurried pace towards equal opportunity for all its citizens has cost generations of Black males a fair chance at achieving the American Dream. Specifically, Black males, throughout American history, due to various forms of systemic racism, have not had as equal an opportunity as White males to access or experience a quality American Life. Ultimately, this has led to a legacy of generations of Black males failing to attain the American Dream.

It is undeniably the moral obligation and responsibility of this Nation to create a culture that is removed of the discriminatory practices that have both historically and presently operated as obstacles on the Black male's path towards the American Dream. This responsibility begins with using psychological science to gain a greater understanding of exactly how racism, stigma, and discrimination influence the mental and emotional functioning of Black males.

What is the Psychology of Racism?

Psychology can be briefly be defined as *the study of how genes and environment affect human thinking, feeling and behavior*. The psychology of racism can be defined as the study of how racism, stigma, and discrimination impact the thinking, feeling and behavior of Black males. In this introductory chapter, I will capture, outline, and summarize the insidious impact of racism, stigma, and discrimination on the psychological functioning of Black males. Furthermore, I will capture, outline, and summarize the intersection between Black males, racial stigma, and their continuing pattern of poor life outcomes.

"A National Emergency"

As we all know, technology and information have come together to make the world both a smaller and more informed place. However as the global community is becoming more informed, Black males are becoming more and more detached from the educational and social processes necessary to thrive in the Age of Information.

So why are we here?

In 1967, Dr. Martin Luther King addressed the American Psychological Association (APA) at its annual convention. During his address, he daringly gave counselors and psychologists the mandate of researching and documenting not only the existence of racism but also the potential negative impact racism may have on the perceptions, emotions, and behaviors of Black Americans.

Specifically, Dr. King stated "America needs to understand that it is poisoned to its soul by racism and this understanding needs to be carefully documented and consequently more difficult to reject". Dr. King understood the ability of racism to be a dynamic force influencing the social progress and moral evolution of American society. Sadly, very few people responded to Dr. King's plea for advocacy through psychological science, as 50 years later only *4%* of psychological research is devoted to understanding the psychological experiences of African Americans. What does this mean? It means that the most vulnerable and embattled portion of the American population currently receives the least amount of evidence-based treatment. Put another way, the highest risk category of American citizens is receiving only minimal amounts of scientific resources.

So where are we now?

It is no mystery that Black males are struggling to achieve upward social mobility. There are mountains of reports and articles that extensively detail the miserable social plight of Black males in America. If you could summarize this mass of statistical evidence into one sentence it would read: "In the United States of America, Black males come in last place on all social measures of success and first place on all social measures of failure". This statistical summation is truly a modern day American tragedy.

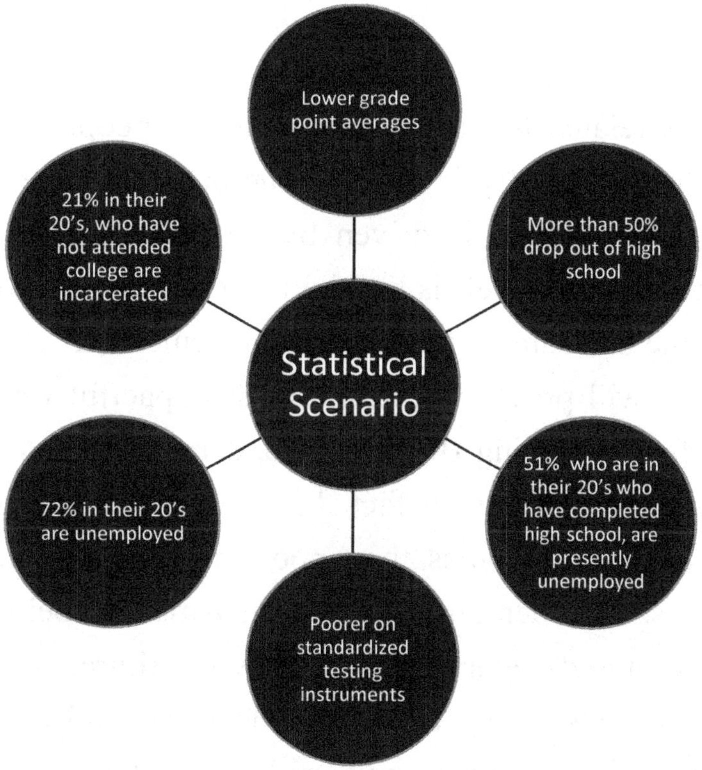

So again, why are we here?

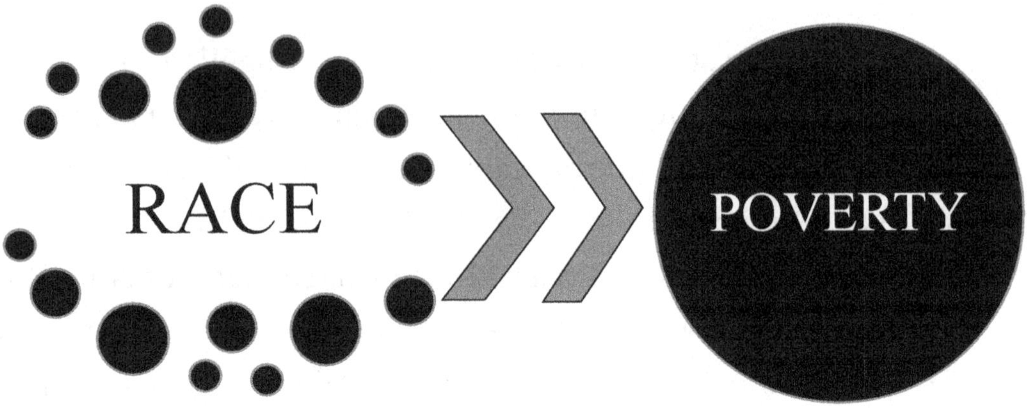

Race > Poverty

As it relates to social failure, many people assume for example, that the epidemic of academic underachievement in the Black male population is driven by poverty. This is a flawed assumption. Poverty itself is not the most impactful variable as it relates to the measure of academic achievement. In contrast, and as this book will prove, race is the most impactful variable as it relates to factors driving Black male underachievement. This can be proven by the statistical fact that poor White males achieve higher academic outcomes than poor, middle, and upper-class Black males. This demonstrates that in America, being a Black male is a seemingly guaranteed pathway to failure. At the end of all social analysis, being a Black male is beyond a shadow of doubt, the single most powerful predictor of academic underachievement and ultimately social failure. In short, race trumps income.

So, if poverty is not the most impactful barrier complicating the academic performance of Black malew, what else could it be?

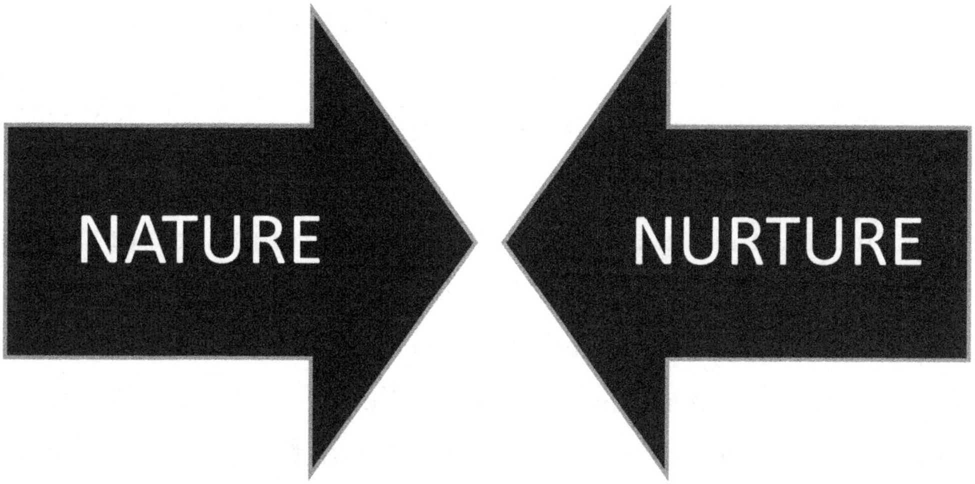

Nature vs. Nurture - Can Black Males be Educated?

If you believe Black males are hereditarily cursed and doomed by *nature*, then you assume that Black males are underperforming academically due to genetic deficiencies. A person with this scientifically constrained viewpoint will perceive any effort made to educate and empower this portion of the American population as a waste of time, money, and other precious social resources. In contrast, if you believe the persistent occurrence of academic underachievement in the Black male population is the result of *nurture*, then you will believe environmental deficits and societal barriers are the essential causes of Black male academic underachievement.

As it relates to the nature explanation for poor academic achievement, genetics can only explain an individual's intellectual capacity. So genetics can place a predetermined ceiling on an individual that prevents a person from summoning the mental power necessary to achieve superior, above average, or even average academic performance. Genetics, however, cannot sufficiently explain underperformance in an area where only an average or even below average level of intellectual ability is necessary for achieving success (i.e. high school diploma).

Thus, when there is no biological explanation for the persistent pattern of academic underachievement on the part of Black males, then there must be an environmental or social explanation for this epidemic which has for so long plagued the Black male population. It can thus be concluded that the epidemic of academic underachievement afflicting the Black male population is not birthed out of genetic deficiency. In a more empirically sound justification, one can conclude that social barriers are producing psychological barriers, which then complicate the ability for Black males to achieve even the minimal required levels of academic achievement.

I will now say in no uncertain terms that genetic structuring does not mediate the relationship between Black males and low academic achievement. In stark contrast, socially-induced psychological barriers are what mediate the relationship between Black males and low academic achievement. What are psychological barriers? Psychological barriers are disempowering thoughts and emotions that restrict performance. Thus, a nurture or social engineering explanation attributes the academic struggles of Black males to psychological struggles, which are rooted in toxic sociocultural experiences encountered during the childhood and adolescent stages of human development.

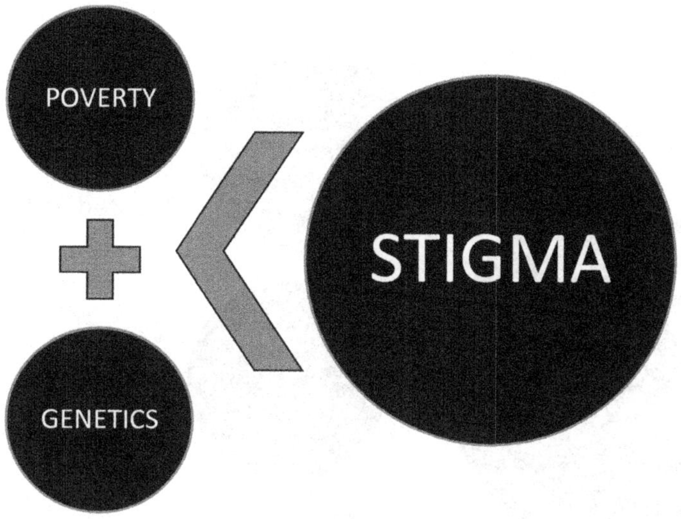

Poverty + Genes = Less Than Toxic Sociocultural Experiences

The Black male represents the most vulnerable and psychologically embattled portion of the American population. What makes the Black male the most psychologically embattled category of American citizen? The answer can be found in the stockpiles of social research that overwhelmingly prove the Black male citizen to be the most hatefully targeted group for discrimination, alienation, objectification, demonization, and humiliation. Thus, due to such stigmatic aggressions, Black males exist psychologically taxed to the point that they lack the internal resources necessary to cover the cost of striving for the American Dream.

The dark summation of the previous paragraphs is that Black males are nurtured in a society where they are branded as incapable, labeled as social liabilities, and expected to fail. They are miseducated to believe their culture and manner of expression is inappropriate, inferior, and irrelevant. They eventually learn and accept that their life in America is regarded as insignificant and unnecessary.

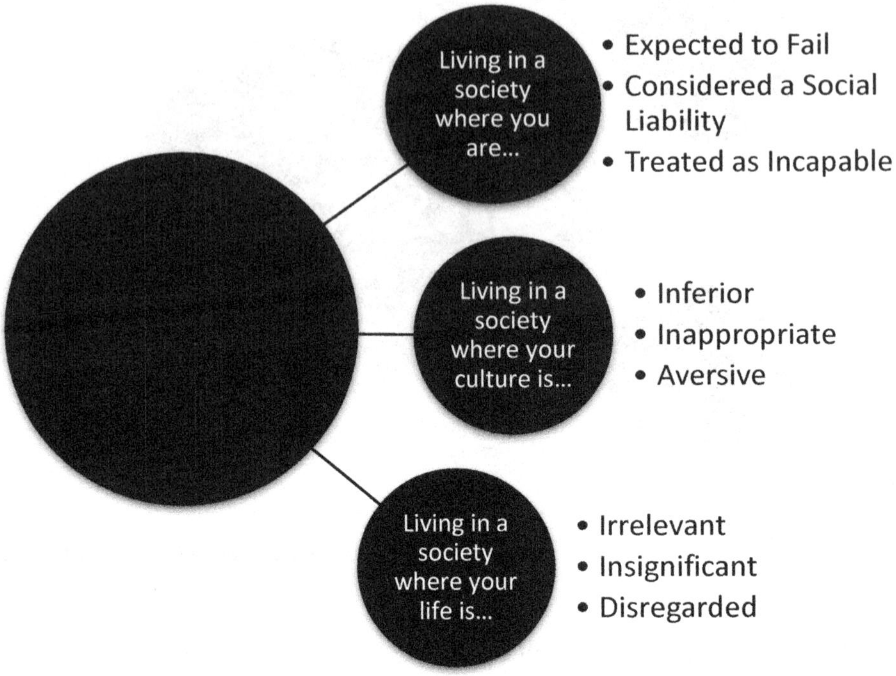

Theory of Causation: Race-Specific Educational Issues are Related to Race-Specific Psychological Issues, Which are Related to Race-Specific Social Experiences

In the adolescent stage of human growth and development, teens are tasked with developing an identity. During these formative years, adolescents experience tumultuous emotions, distorted perceptions, and confusing biological changes. In this stage of psychological sensitivity and emotional vulnerability, Black males are systematically indoctrinated by an ideology that propagates the idea that Black males are inferior, incapable, and destined for failure. Research has consistently demonstrated that Black male youth are targeted for social stigma more than any other category of American citizens (even Black male adults). Sadly and consequently, at a very early age, Black male youth understand that the world views them because of their appearance, through a perpetual lens of negativity and repulsion

This consistent pattern of inferiorizing communication comes during a time when a young maturing mind lacks the psychological sophistication, life experience, and level of brain development required to engage in the level of critical thinking necessary to guard against the internalization of these negative messages. More times than not, this lack of an effective psychological defense system in the face of a relentless and unavoidable stigmatizing messaging system, leads to destructive internalization, which ultimately leads to their eventual failure.

During the identity forming years, the egocentric adolescent brain believes life revolves around him and he is on the world's stage being judged, critiqued, and defined. During this profoundly impressionable stage, Black boys are being tragically racialized and stigmatized to the point that psychological exhaustion is inevitable. In the end, we now as a society, are left to pick up the tab on the cost of underperformance from a category of American citizens who were socially engineered for failure. Note: If you put 100 White boys through these same psyche and identity shaping experiences, they would attain the same statistical results as Black boys.

Race-Based Psychosocial Engineering

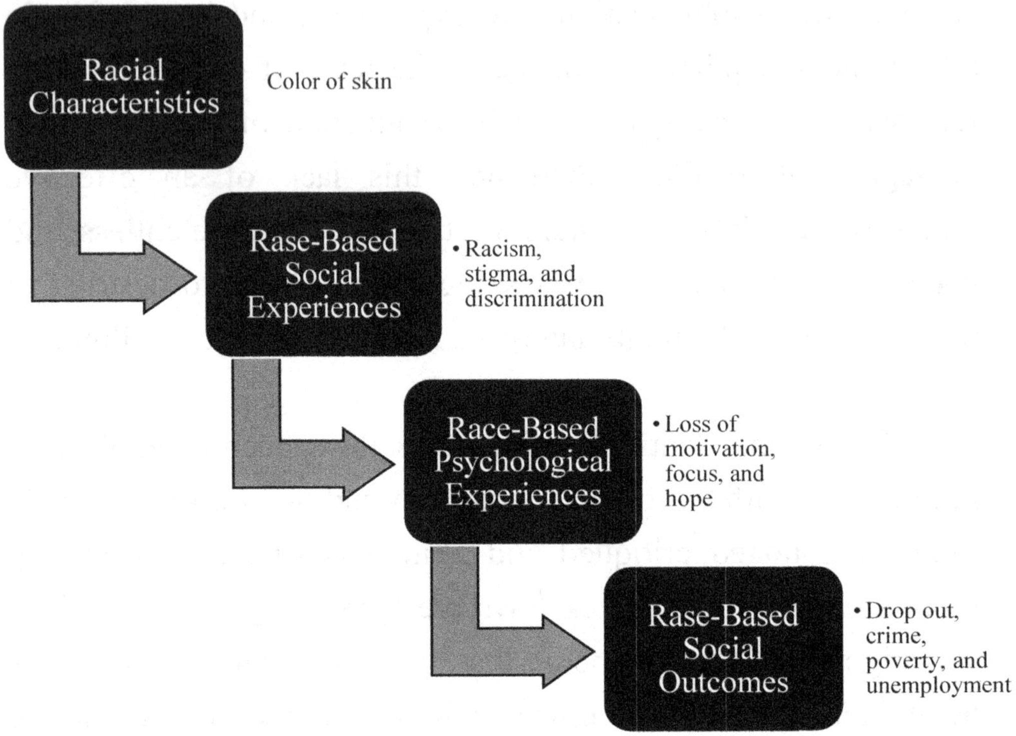

Race and Reason: The Necessary Conditions for a Racist Society

The blessing of living in a racially-diverse society is that we have the opportunity to interact with a rainbow of individuals of varying races, cultures, customs, traditions, languages, and worldviews. The curse that accompanies living in a racially-diverse society is that with its multiracial make-up comes the reality of racism. What is racism? Racism is fundamentally defined as the belief that one category of people who have a shared physical appearance is superior to another category of people who have a shared physical appearance. As a result of race and human nature, America functions as a hyper color-conscious and color-driven society.

Living in a racially-divided society, we are systematically socialized to cognitively and emotionally internalize the biases and stereotypes that saturate American society. These stereotypes and biases consistently manifest themselves consciously and subconsciously through our thoughts and behaviors in our everyday lives.

Due to our human tendencies to 1. Experience survival related fear, 2. Be socially competitive and 3. Naturally gravitate towards people with whom we have shared physical characteristics - *racism is inevitable.* As it relates to the survival of the fittest, we are always competing for resources. We naturally assume "I am more likely to survive if I have more resources". Furthermore, we naturally assume "I am likely to have more resources if I work with other people". Thus when it comes to picking teammates in this "race for resources" we are naturally more likely to pick people who look like us or who are already wearing the same color uniform (i.e. skin color). Ultimately, as a result of race and human nature, America is wired to be a color-conscious and color-driven society.

Black Barriers are White Forts

No matter how dead or imaginary the system of racism may seem, it is alive and active and its ability to influence our present and future society is undeniable. Majority supremacy of past centuries still trickles its influence into today's society. The race-driven class hierarchy established centuries ago, even today, still dictate who has access to prearranged race-based social accommodations.

As a result of racism, stigma, and discrimination - *success is not solely a by-product of individual ability, drive, intelligence, ingenuity, etc*. In America, success is a by-product of prearranged privilege and accommodating conditions given to certain members of society. Just as past earthquakes, volcanoes, tornadoes, etc. are responsible for present-day natural environments, in like manner, past policies, procedures, and societal mechanisms are responsible for modern-day social and cultural conditions.

The Myth of a Post-Racial America

Racism and a lack of education have worked together since the beginning of American history, to function as the two most derailing barriers to Black Americans. Even more, the spirit of racism combined with restricted educational opportunities, have historically placed Black youth in vulnerable social positions. All this being said, before we can interrogate the spirit of racism, we will first statistically prove its existence. The following is a brief outline and summary of the statistical gaps that clearly prove the presence of systemic racism in the educational, occupational, and judicial systems of American society. These three individual systems of American society represent the most critical and necessary components as it relates to an individual's ability to achieve upward social mobility.

Before I provide statistical evidence for the existence of racism, I will use the next page to quickly define several key terms relevant to the remainder of this book.

Key Definitions

Race - A class of people categorized by their shared physical appearance.
(i.e. "how they look")

Racial Prejudice - To hold negative preconceived opinions and attitudes about a race of people.
(i.e. "I hate being around those type of people. They are so ignorant")

Racism - The belief that one category of people who have a shared physical appearance is superior to another category of people who have a shared physical appearance
(i.e. "people who look like me are better than people who look like you")

Racial Stigma - When a class of people are collectively inferiorized by other members of society because of how they look
(i.e. "people like that are genetically inferior and are a liability to our great Country")

Racial Discrimination - The strategic and systematic practice of unfairly manipulating and minimizing the flow of social resources to people of a specific racial category
(i.e. "I will do whatever I can [covertly or overtly] to never hire, include, support, or provide opportunities to those people")

Miseducated Minds: Racism in America's Education System

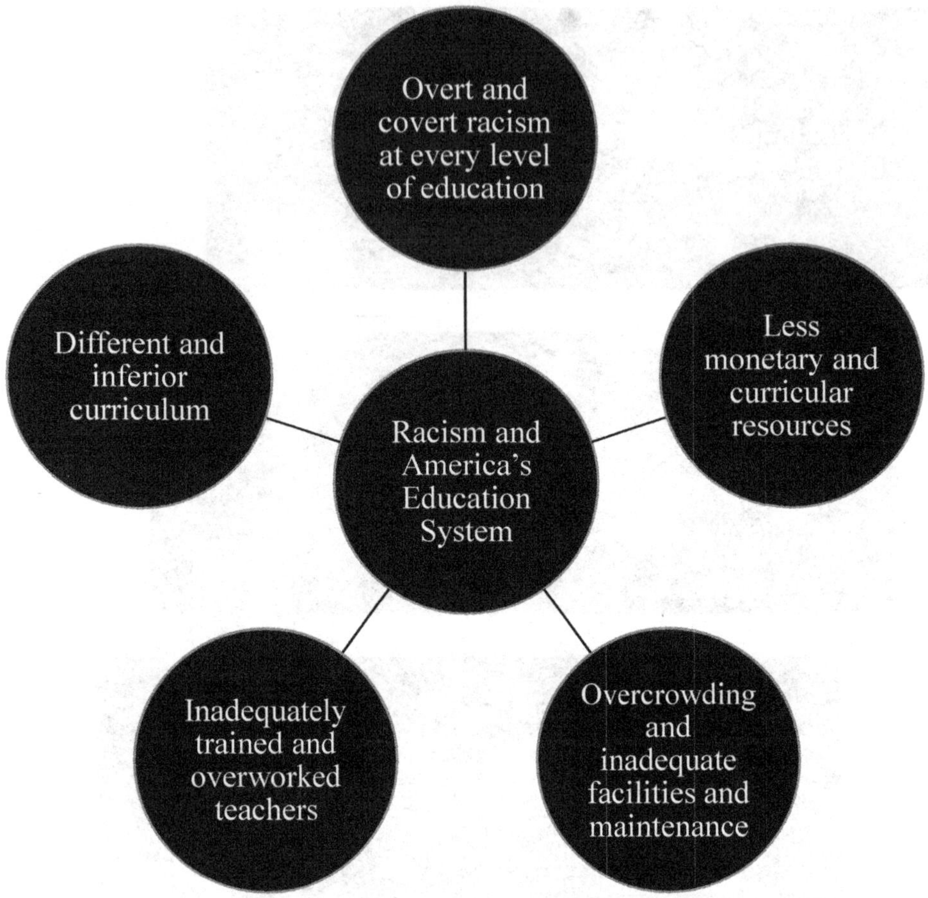

Throughout the history of America, race-based educational oppression has disrupted the academic progress of Black youth. In present day society, the majority of a Black male youth's experiences with racism will occur in the school setting. A multitude of researchers have suggested that systemic racism pervades every aspect and level of the educational process. Statistically speaking, since the birth of our Country, fewer monetary and curricular resources have been allocated to educate Black students. Furthermore, schools that Black males typically attend are often characterized by overcrowding, inadequate maintenance, inadequately trained teachers, overworked teachers, and inferior curriculums. What makes this reality even more unsettling is that the young developing minds subjugated to these discriminatory educational settings are consciously aware of and expectant of such racial practices in the school systems in which they are being educated.

Research has further confirmed that White teachers have the propensity to present inaccurate or biased information to Black male students and are also more likely to unfairly evaluate their Black male students. Examiners have also observed that Black male students are more likely to be labeled as mentally retarded and are suspended and/or expelled from school at an alarmingly higher rate than White male students. In every chapter of American history, Black males have been susceptible to encountering systematic barriers that complicate their ability to attain a sufficient level of education. This susceptibility of encountering racially-constructed educational barriers is thoroughly documented and empirically undeniable.

Imprisoning Potential: Institutional Racism in America's Justice System

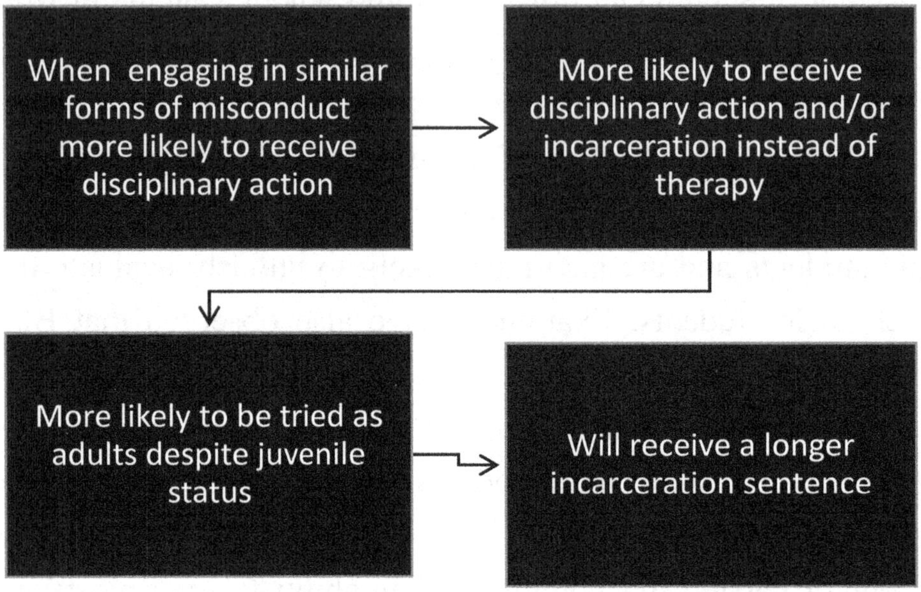

Neuroscientists have clearly described the slower brain development of males, in comparison to females, specifically when it comes to frontal lobe development. The frontal lobe is the area of the brain responsible for executive functioning (i.e. impulse control, critical thinking, and decision making). As a result of slower brain development, boys in general are more likely to engage in risk-taking, impulsive behavior, bad decision-making, and other forms of externalizing behaviors. Despite this universal truth, research has consistently demonstrated that White male youth in comparison to Black male youth are more likely to receive preferential treatment from the judicial system.

History vividly outlines the unyielding maltreatment of Black males by the judicial system of America. Throughout the span of the past 500 years, kidnapping, lynching, police brutality, and unfair prison sentences have characterized the Black males' experience with the legal system of America. Even in modern times, Black males have been seemingly marginalized and targeted for maltreatment by the justice system of America. In general, Black males are at an increased risk of having negative encounters with law enforcement agencies. Furthermore, when engaging in similar forms of misconduct, studies have found that Black males (adolescents and adults) are more drastically punished than White males (adolescent and adults). Even deeper and more disheartening is the statistical reality that Black male adolescents are more likely to receive disciplinary action and/or incarceration instead of culturally relevant therapeutic interventions when navigating through the justice system.

Withouy any shadow of doubt, these previously mentioned injustices are responsible for the U.S. Surgeon General report indicating that Black males are overwhelmingly overrepresented in the American prison system. It is a glaringly gross statistical imbalance that although Black males make up only 6% of the United States population, they represent 49% of the United States prison system. Finally, although Black youth only make up 6% of America's youth population (ages 10-17), they represent 32% of America's juvenile system.

According to U.S. Census Bureau data, the percentage of Black males incarcerated (12%) was only slightly less than the percentage of Black males who had obtained a college degree (13%). Also, researchers have consistently documented that in contrast to White males, Black males are more likely to receive longer incarceration sentences, more likely to be tried as adults despite juvenile status, and more likely to receive capital punishment sentences for crimes committed against White Americans than for crimes committed against Black Americans.

These glaring statistical accounts of the unequal treatment of Black males by the judicial system of America are undeniable and unignorably obvious. The Black male's added task of psychologically navigating the threats and obstacles placed on his path by the legal system is, arguably an operative distraction to social achievement.

The statistics presented above vividy prove that the American judicial system functions in a way in which Black boys are more likely, due to inequality, to incur a criminal record. This socially propelled propensity to attain a criminal record at a young age will ultimately result in Black men encountering difficulty attaining housing and employment. Such early-life inequalities will later in life serve as barriers to the collective ability of the Black Male population to achieve upward mobility in American society.

Dollars and Sense: Systemic Racism in America's Labor Force

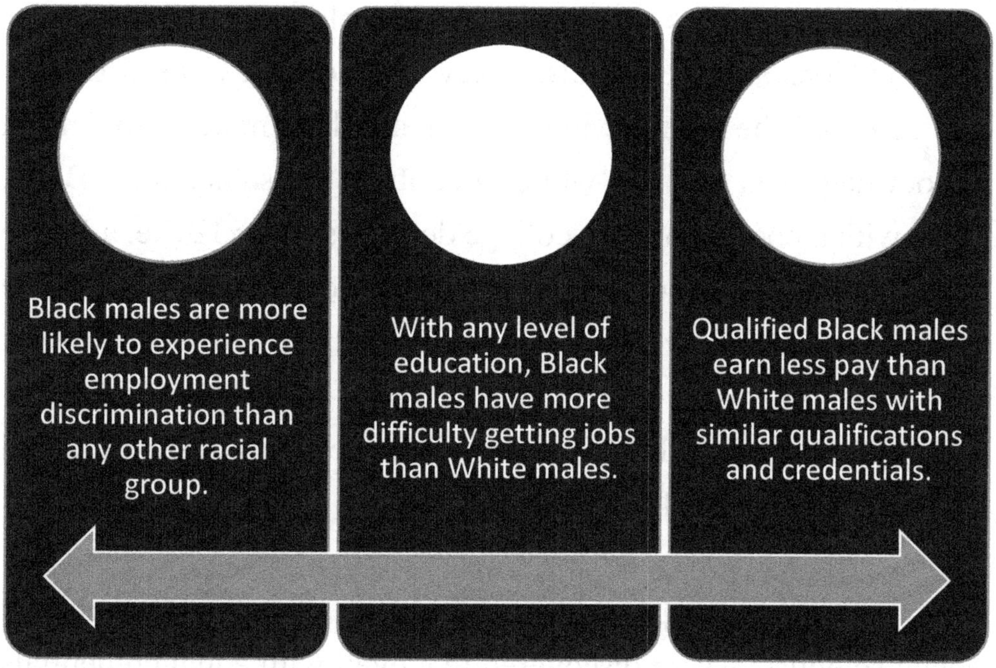

From the days of slavery, to the era of 40 acres and a mule, to the modern day practice of racially-profiling employment applications, Black males have been notoriously exploited by America's labor system. In contemporary American society, Black males have been found to experience employment discrimination more than any other racial group. It has become common knowledge in America that Black males have more difficulty obtaining employment than their White male peers. This is most likely indicative of U.S. Census Bureau data that reports Black males to be two times more likely to be unemployed in comparison to White males. In further revealing statistics, 72% of Black male high school dropouts are unemployed in comparison to 34% of White male high school dropouts. The U.S. Surgeon General also found that Black males experience more instances of prolonged periods of unemployment than White males.

Finally, in regards to evidence of systemic racism in America's labor force, researchers have found that qualified Black males still earn less pay than White males who have similar qualifications and credentials. Likewise, the U.S. Census Bureau has reported the average income for a White male with a high school degree is $17,583 while in contrast the salary for a Black male with a post-secondary college degree is $16,532 (i.e. a White male with a high school diploma makes more than a Black male with a post-secondary degree). Researchers have further uncovered that Black male college graduates have an average salary of $31,000 per year, while White male college graduates attained average salaries of $40,000 per year.

Even more exposing are the results of recent research by social scientists which discovered that even with equal credentials and qualifications presented on a resume, people with "Black sounding names" are dramatically less likely to receive interview offers in comparison to people with "White sounding names". Such statistical findings serve as compelling evidence that the practices of systemic racism still pervade numerous levels of America's labor structuring. In summary, the American labor system is structured in a manner in which Black males are less likely to receive invitations for a job interview, less likely to receive job offers, and prone to receive less pay for equal work despite equal or higher qualifications and credentials.

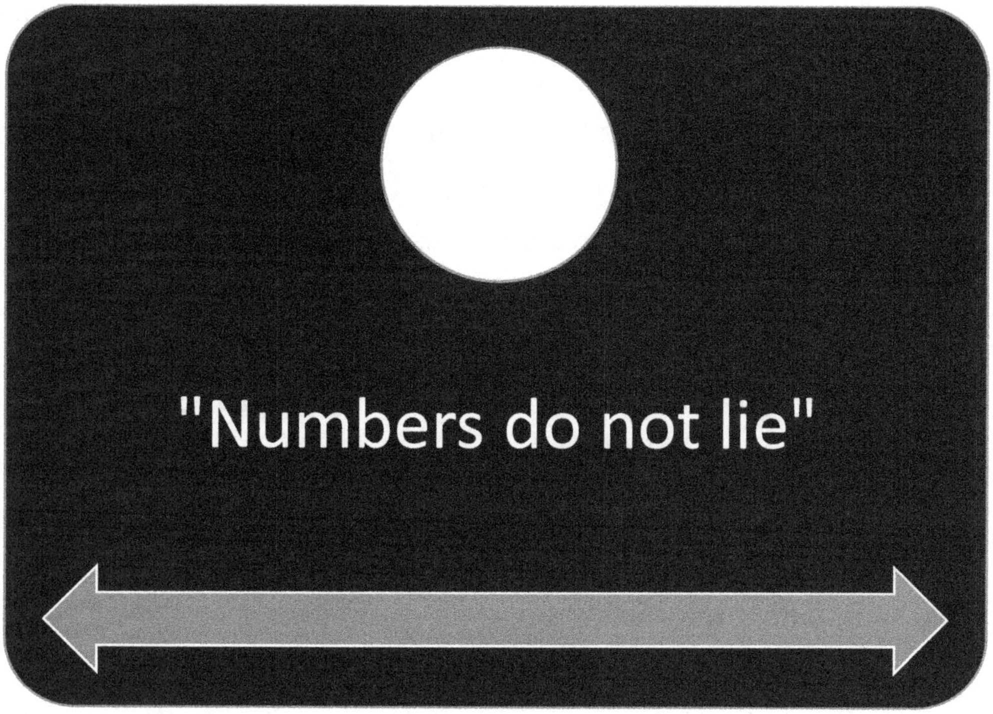

Systemic Racism: Alive and Active

This chapter, in only a few paragraphs, has proven that various forms of systemic racism in America have served the purpose of providing advantageous privileges to its White male citizens and disadvantageous circumstances to its Black male citizens. In a short statistical review, it has been scientifically proven that racially-discriminatory practices in American society have a negative impact on the social mobility and social well-being of Black males. The presence and effects of systemic racism on the Black male experience is both appalling and unacceptable.

As children go through the adolescent stage, they become more aware of the economic, social, and political mechanisms situated in society that will serve as potential barriers during their life journey. The young developing minds subjugated to these inequitable social circumstances are consciously aware of and perceptually expectant of racial prejudice and discrimination.

As with all people, a Black male's motivation to succeed is directly related to his perceptions of whether or not his hard work and dedication will lead to his realization of the American Dream. As previously mentioned, researchers have found that Black males perceive academic achievement as benefiting only White Americans. This perspective is most likely the result of a Black male youth becoming aware of the centuries of strategic discriminatory practices that have limited and/or denied deserving individuals from the Black racial group access to varying jobs and positions in society. In short, they are not seeing (historically or presently) hard work, dedication, and small successes pay off for those with whom they share the same racial group.

It is this bleak awareness that slowly compels Black male youth to become disillusioned to the American Dream. Social scientists have found that in comparison to Black female students, Black males are even more likely, for example, to perceive school as a "waste of time". This finding may be indicative of other research that has found that Black male students put less energy and effort into academic pursuits and also attain lower grade point averages than Black female students.

America: Sweet Mother Dearest

America is the epitome of a bad or dead-beat mother. Mother America is raising two separate categories of children. Although these children live in the same house they are raised by two totally different forms of parental guidance. One child is given positive information about who he is and what the future holds. The other child is given negative messages about who he is and what the future holds. One child is fully accepted and routinely affirmed through empowering messaging. To this child, America embodies hope, opportunity, and nurturance. The other child, in stark contrast, is consistently given discouraging and non-affirming messages. To this child, America embodies doubt, inequality, and neglect.

At the end of the day, Mother America, like the classic bad parent, will say that it does not understand why the rejected child "can't seem to get it together". Mother America will say, "my other child is thriving so it can't be because of how I raised them since they both lived in the same house under the same rules". The typical bad parent, just like American racism, will in personal defense, boldly look into the eyes of their now disempowered adult child and declare, "What I said and did to you has nothing to do with who you have become".

Who Am I? The World is a Stage

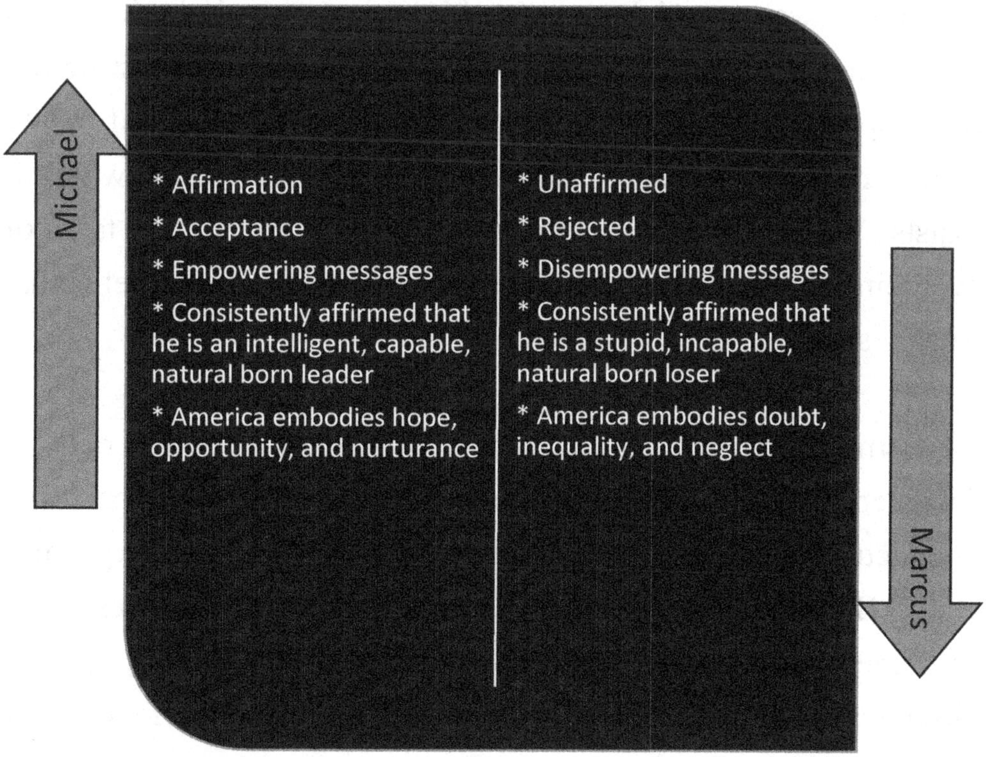

During the Identity Formation years, the egocentric adolescent brain perceives the world as a stage. To the Black male adolescent, the audience of his life views him through a lens of negativity, aversion, and repulsion. Rejection is arguably the most psychologically impactful human experience. It in my personal belief that rejection leaves an even greater psychological indentation than love. Over time, a Black boy's sustained exposure to mass racialized rejection has a cumulative impact that eventually equates to social traumatization. This accumulated trauma, at the most profound of levels, negatively affects the identity development of the Black male adolescent.

People in general have extreme difficulty accepting, handling, and coping with rejection. As a psychologist, I would approximate that 80% of the people I see in therapy are seeking therapy due to past, present, or anticipated experiences of rejection. By nature we are all born with biological, psychological, and intellectual strengths and weaknesses. America's social structure is set up in a way in which the psychological strengths of White males are maximized. It is further set-up in a manner in which it assists White males via affirming messaging, in the task of overcoming their biological, psychological, and intellectual weaknesses.

In definitive contrast, America's social environment is designed to erode away at the biological, psychological, and intellectual strengths of the Black male. This eroding away of a young Black male's natural strengths simultaneously takes place as American culture insidiously maximizes and triggers the biological, psychological, and intellectual weaknesses of the Black male.

Again, the Black male is viewed by the rest of the world through a lens of negativity. This mass rejection and inferiorizing is most assaultive during the formative adolescent years. The adolescent years, as we all know, are the most emotionally draining years of human growth and development. This formative period is a time when identity is being formed, emotions are exaggerated, and perceptions are jaded. Such large scale social rejection during an extremely psychologically sensitive period, no doubt brings a dark cloud of despair over the hearts and minds of developing Black boys. These young mind lack the psychological sophistication necessary to block the internalization of society's negative attitudes, beliefs, and perspectives of Black males. Ultimately, these young minds begin the slow process of stigma identification and internalization.

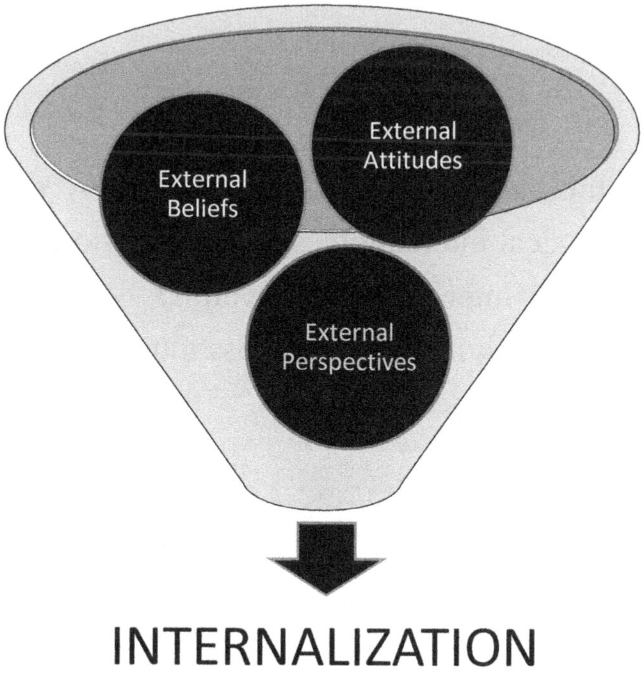

The Eight Stages of Stigma Immersion and Stigma Internalization (SISI)

Stigmatizing information is transmitted and reinforced through a system of inferiorizing cultural messaging and prejudicial social interactions. These stigmatizing messages and interactions are systematic and mechanical in nature. Over time, the relentless circulation of stigmatic messages in American culture overpowers the young Black American Dreamer and the process of internalization begins.

The next few pages outline the eight stage process of Stigma Immersion and Internalization (SISI). I developed this model to conceptualize, capture, and outline the process by which young Black boys systematically internalize society's negative beliefs, perceptions, and attitudes about the Black male.

Stage 1
Exposure and Experiences

During this stage, the developing Black boy will encounter routine psychological interactions with the inferiorizing messages and stigmatizing interactions pervading American culture (Example: "As a Black male you are less intelligent and are prone to failure")

Stage 2
Resilience and Rejection

During this stage a Black boy will display an initial reflexive rejection or denial of the inferiorizing messages and/or social interactions (Example: "No I will not fail. I am an intelligent person who is destined to do great things in life!")

Stage 3
Cognitive Dissonance

During this stage, consistent negative messaging produces an internal argument or debate as to whether or not the stigmatic messages about the self are true or false (Example: "I can do anything I put my mind to…well maybe I will end up going to prison…no that is not my destiny, I refuse to be a statistic!")

Stage 4
Stigma Reinforcement

During this critical stage, the young developing mind begins to consciously and subconsciously scan reality and interpret life experiences through a lens of powerlessness, shame, and impending failure (Example: "Why am I having so much trouble in school? Maybe I should get it over with and drop out". "Why do police officers constantly stare at me when they drive past? Maybe I should act like a criminal.")

Stage 5
Relinquishment and Acceptance

During this stage, a young Black boy decreases his allocation of psychological energy he uses to block stigma internalization. This leads to a slow acceptance and personal agreement with society's dooming social prophecy (Example: "I'm so tired of people treating me like a dumb criminal. If that's who everyone thinks I am I might as well be that person. Ain't nobody really trying to help me be successful anyway.")

Stage 6
Internalization and Identification

During this terrible stage, a Black boy absorbs and integrates the stigmatizing messages into his mental model and system of identity. (Example: "Man I ain't going to college…that's for White people. The "real niggas" I know getting paid by any means necessary." "Man I ain't got time to waste trying to graduate. I know sooner or later either the police are gonna try to put me in jail or somebody will not give me a job because I'm Black.")

Stage 7
Disassociated Belief-System, Value-System, and Self-System

At this stage of disengagement, a Black boy separates himself from typical American values as it relates to what it takes to achieve the American Dream (example: "A Black man like me will never get a fair shot at a good job. The only way I can get ahead is to connect with the guys running these streets and making things happen. They get respect. Better yet, maybe I should focus on being a rapper or a basketball player. It seems like that is how most Black guys make it in America.")

Stage 8
Stigmatic Psychosocial Functioning

At this pre-failure stage, a Black boy utilizes dysfunctional coping strategies to deal with the uncomfortable emotions brought on by national rejection and stigma (example: Self-Sabotage: habitually creating problems that will serve as an excuse to escape responsibility on put forth a full effort)

Symptoms of Stigma Internalization

Cognitive Symptoms

- Disempowered Mental Model (interpreting, framing, organizing, and filtering reality through a lens of limitation, inequality, and fear)
- Vulnerability Informed Perspective (lack of racial capital i.e. "Because I am Black, the world will not be fair and life will be harder for me.")
- Dysfunctional Negative Schema (automatic negative thoughts, schema affirming negative associations, and disempowering cognitive distortions)

Emotional Symptoms

- Disempowering Emotions (intrusive negative affect, hopelessness, anxiety, and fear)

Behavioral Symptoms

- Counterproductive Coping (externalizing behavior, escaping behaviors, problematic decision-making, and troublesome interpersonal interactions)

Self-View: The Black Male Adolescent's Perception of Self

It is scientifically proven that people who belong to a social group that is devalued, underprivileged, and discriminated against, are more likely to experience poor self-esteem, feelings of worthlessness, self-hatred, and negative attitudes toward the self and the social group in which they belong. It can thus be theorized that Black boys are at an increased risk of internalizing mainstream society's stigmatizing messaging and eventually develop negative attitudes and perceptions about themselves.

World-View: The Black Male Adolescent's Perception of a Racist American System

Many Black males report racism to be a primary life stressor. Black males routinely report experiencing racially-charged messages and interactions in educational, political, legal, occupational, and social settings. These messages and interactions erode at the psychological structuring of the young Black male. Stigmatizing messages about one's self, combined with a fear triggering awareness of American discrimination, strips away the dignity, self-efficacy, and self-respect of young Black boys.

To perceive the self as living in a culture in which one's unique potentials and viewpoints are not genuinely and sincerely valued, respected, and celebrated can leave a person feeling irrelevant, invaluable, and socially unnecessary. Individuals developing in such a climate often begin to align their thinking, feeling, and behavior to mainstream society's racist messages, stereotypes, and expectations. This psychological alignment hinders a Black male's pursuit of becoming a productive and relevant member of society. Consequently, these young minds are at an increased risk of experiencing negative life outcomes.

Life-View: The Black Male Teen's Pessimistic Attitude toward the Future

Black males often have difficulty believing hard work pays off and anyone can get ahead in life regardless of their race. Such fatalistic assumptions are likely connected to a young boy's slowly increasing awareness of the potential for people of his racial group to be treated unfairly.

The Trinity of Failure: A Gloomy Intersection of Self, World, and Future

In summary, it could be theorized that a Black male adolescent is likely to internalize the country's messages of inferiority and as a result develop a negative self-image. Furthermore this same individual due to a history of American racism, will perceive that the world is racist, discriminatory, and unfair. Because of these previously mentioned assumptions, this young Black boy will automatically generate negative views about his ability to positively influence his future and in particular the futility of engaging in academic pursuits.

Combining these three potential mind-sets (a) negative perceptions of self, (b) perceptions of living in an unfair society and (c) a pessimistic outlook on the future, one can understand how these three cognitive assumptions can collectively function to produce emotionally taxing situations in which any individual would be desperate to escape. It could thus be theorized that an adolescent aged Black male who belongs to a historically stigmatized group, will more than likely anticipate unavoidable and uncontrollable encounters with racism. This justifiable negative outlook on the future could then be theorized to cause a Black male adolescent to see the world in a way that reinforces his perceptions and assumptions of an impending state of failure. A brief description of this 3-dimensional framework for failure is outlined on the following page.

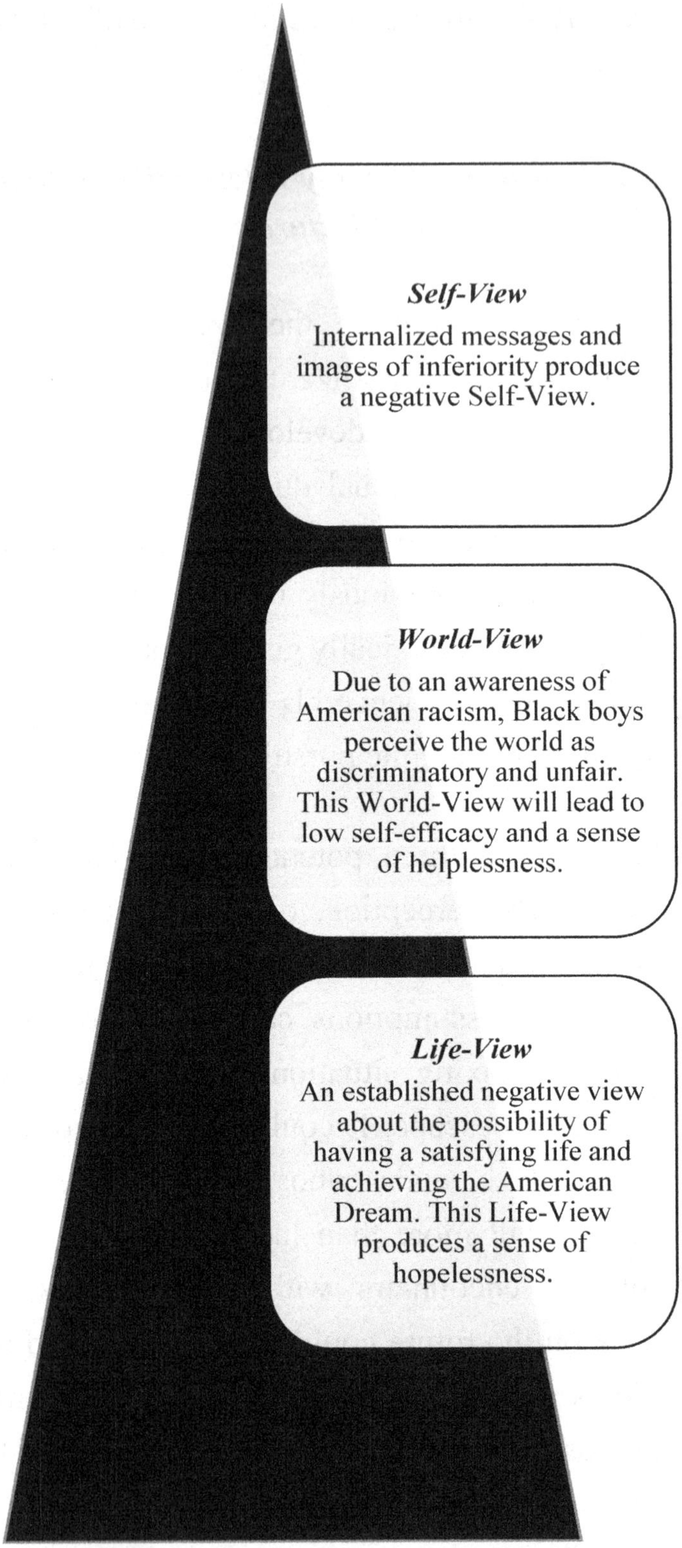
Self-View
Internalized messages and images of inferiority produce a negative Self-View.
World-View
Due to an awareness of American racism, Black boys perceive the world as discriminatory and unfair. This World-View will lead to low self-efficacy and a sense of helplessness.
Life-View
An established negative view about the possibility of having a satisfying life and achieving the American Dream. This Life-View produces a sense of hopelessness.

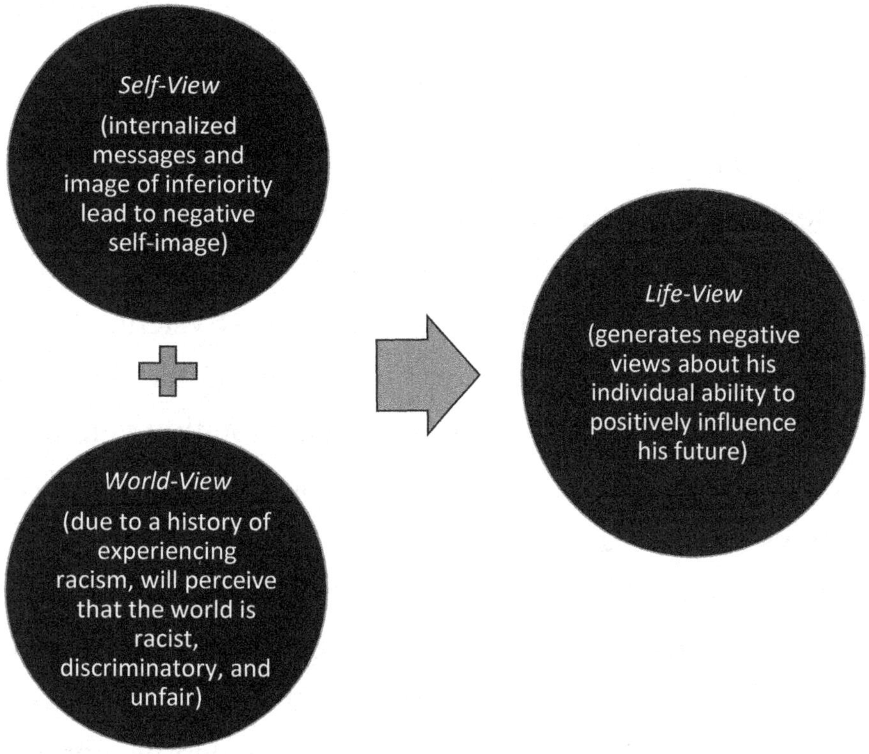

A Framework for Failure

We live in a race-sensitive, race-driven, and racially-divided society. In our racialized culture, Black males are treated on a national level, as the lowest category of American citizens. This engulfing social reality causes Black boys to be incapable of escaping or avoiding routine exposures to inferiorizing communication. So starting from a blank slate, the building blocks of the Black boy's Belief-System (belief about self, life, and future), Value-System (what matters, what he is personally responsible for, and what is respectable) and Self-System (personal sense of efficacy, esteem, and image) are stigma and rejection. These building blocks of stigma and rejection become infrastructures of hopelessness which will evolve into a jaded Belief-System (internally or externally incapable of attaining the American Dream), a socially ineffective Value-System (misguided motivations), and a disempowered Self-System (no power, no value, and no dignity).

My theory on the Psychology of Racism is guided by the principle that the Self-View, World-View, and Life View serve as the building blocks of the Belief-System, Value-System, and Self-System. The resulting Belief-System, Value-System, and Self-System work together to determine perceptions. Perceptions ultimately determine one's response system. With this in mind, it can be theorized that as a result of destructive internalization, Black boys psychologically evolve into Black men who perceive themselves, the world, life and the future through a perceptual lens of negativity, rejection, and alienation. Ultimately, in the face of situations or challenges that require hope, the hopeless Black male is statistically more likely to respond with maladaptive coping (i.e. escapism, avoidance, and self-sabotage). If these young minds are not re-conditioned, re-engineered, re-built, and re-programmed, the reality of massive amounts of poor life outcomes amongst Black males will sadly continue. The diagram below illustrates how racism, stigma and discrimination negatively impact the Self, Belief, and Value systems of the Black male psyche.

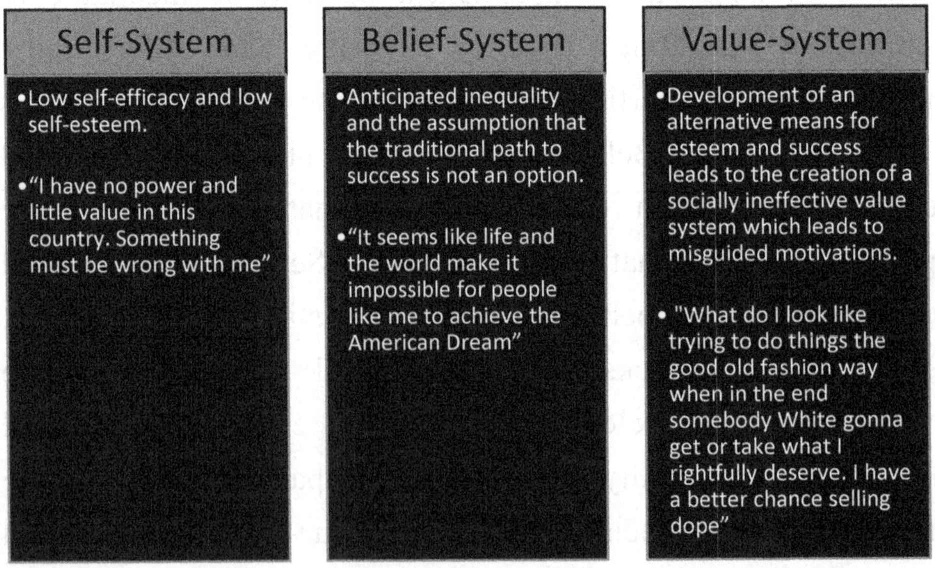

SECTION II.

Excuse or Explanation? An Answer to the Cause of Black Male Underachievement

The Psychology of Racism 2

Excuse or Explanation? An Answer to the Cause of Black Male Underachievement

Deep History – Deep Troubles

The societal purpose of racial discrimination is to limit access and unfairly distribute resources to persons belonging to specific racial groups. The trinity of racism, stigma, and discrimination has created deep histories of failure, disappointment, vulnerability, poverty, set-backs, and unmet socio-emotional needs for Black males. Young Black minds have slowly but surely prepared themselves for failure and have subconsciously given themselves permission to live out the social prophecy that has haunted them since a very young age. In a seemingly automatic manner, these weary minds consciously as well as subconsciously look for signs of failure and opportunities for escape. They become followers of the stigmatic voice that has been whispering defeat in their ears for essentially all their lives.

Race-Related Stress

Researchers have found that in comparison to other racial minority groups, Black males report higher levels of psychological stress as a result of exposure to racism. This could be the result of related research which asserts that due to distinctly differing physical characteristics, Black males are more susceptible to experiencing racially-motivated forms of discrimination than all other minority groups. For Black males, intense barrages of stigmatic messaging (like a city full of demoralizing billboards) creates a maze of anxiety provoking messages, interactions, and situations.

Why Are Experiences of Racism So Stressful?

The experience of stress arises as a result of exposure to, or anticipated exposure to, threatening stimuli. According to the Hobfoll Theory of Stress, stress is produced within the psychological functioning of an individual when (a) an individual's resources are threatened with loss, (b) an individual experiences loss of resources, and/or (c) an individual fails to gain sufficient resources following significant resource investment. Applying this theory of stress, race-related stress could be conceptualized as the psychological consequence of constantly perceiving that due to your racial characteristics, your personal resources or access to resources will be minimized, withheld, or taken away.

Race-related stress has been described by Philomena Essed in this manner: "to live with the threat of racism means planning, almost every day of one's life, how to avoid or defend oneself against discrimination". Such planning, anticipation, and attempts at avoidance and/or defense are common physical and psychological tasks for Black male youth. This type of a seemingly omnipresent threat of discrimination, without question, produces conscious and subconscious stress within the minds of Black male adolescents and Black male adults.

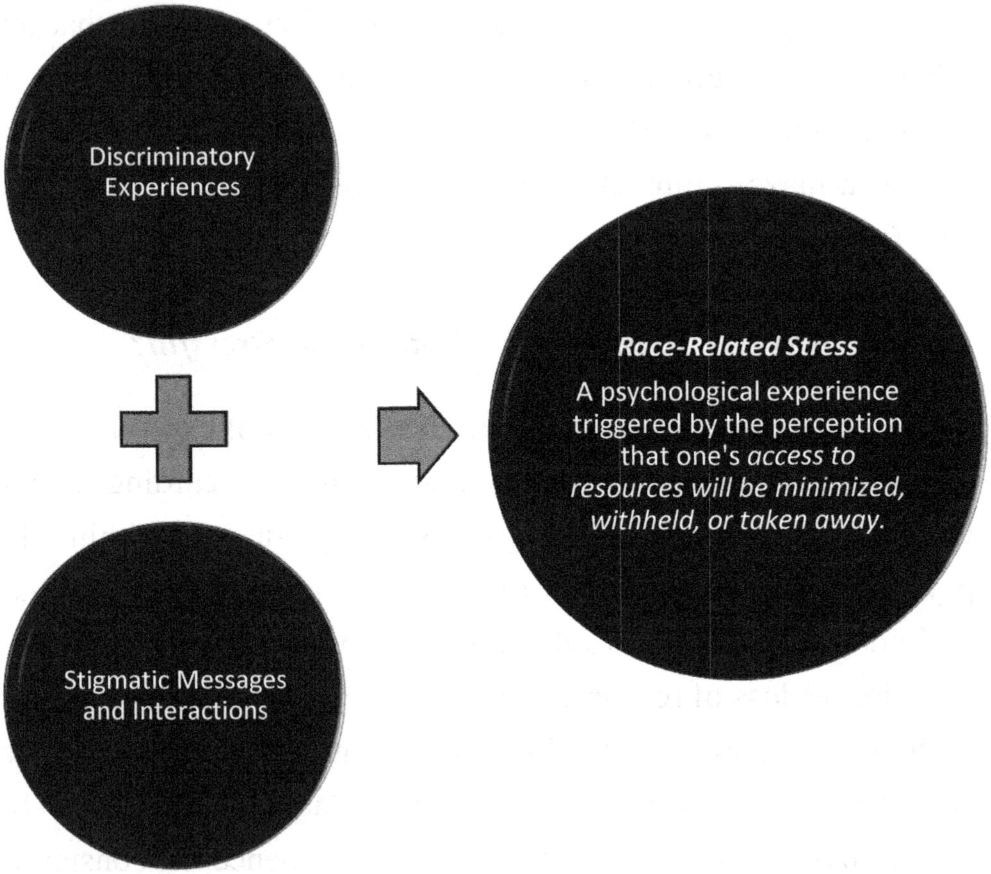

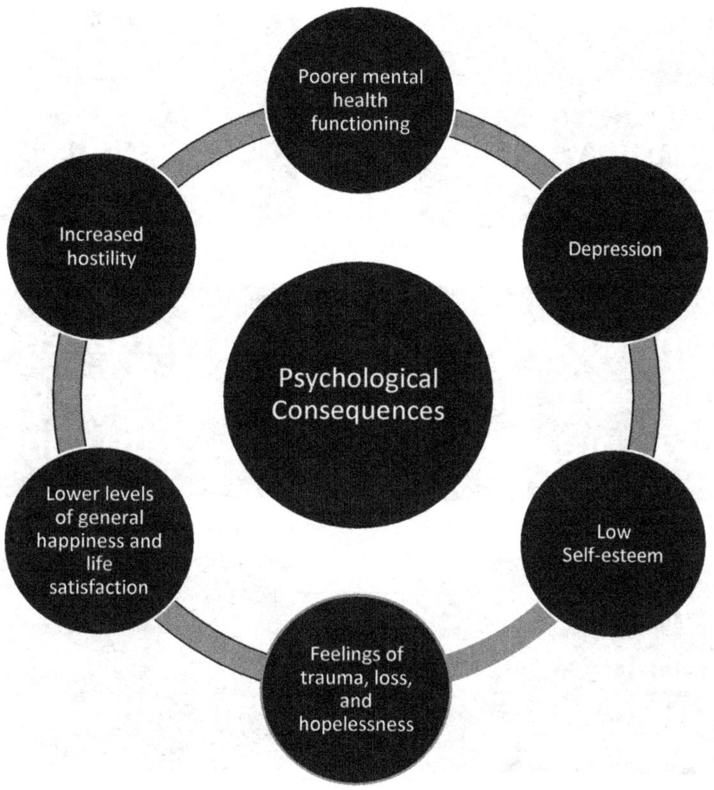

The Psychological Consequences of Race-Related Stress

Black males are immersed in an atmosphere circulating with racially-threatening stimuli. These young minds are essentially unguarded and eventually susceptible to experiencing race-related stress symptoms.

Past researchers have empirically proven an inextricable link between race-related stress and psychological distress (e.g. poorer mental health functioning, lowered self-esteem, feelings of trauma, loss, helplessness, lowered levels of general happiness, and increased hostility). The consistently established connection between race-related stress and psychological dysfunction warrants the assumption that American racism, stigma, and discrimination are insidiously connected to the continuing trend of Black male underachievement.

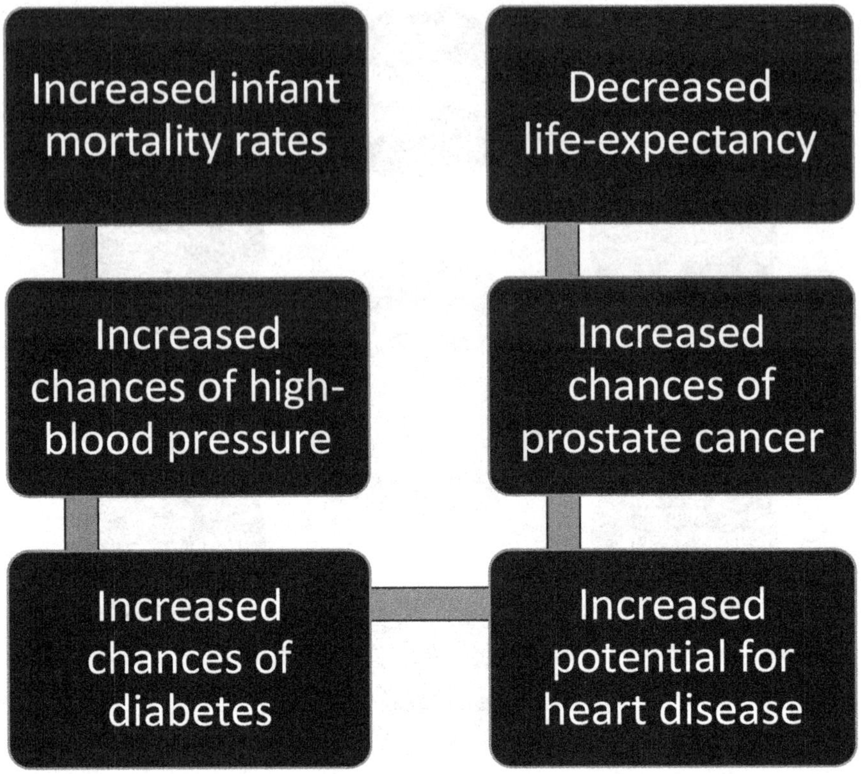

The Physiological Consequences of Race-Related Stress

The effects of race-related stress have been demonstrated to go beyond the boundaries of psychological functioning. Race-related stress insidiously invades the physical health of Black males. Numerous studies have found race-related stress to cause numerous health issues. The ability of race-related stress to increase health-related issues could be indicative of a report issued by the Centers for Disease Control National Center for Health Statistics, which reported that Blacks experience increased mortality rates, decreased life-expectancy, and increased potentials for heart disease, diabetes, breast cancer, and prostate cancer. Furthermore, race-related stress has also been found to be empirically linked to the onset of high-blood pressure and cardiovascular disease. The previously mentioned empirical evidence clearly illustrates the ability of race-related stress to infect and weaken the physical health of Blacks males living in America….from the cradle to the grave.

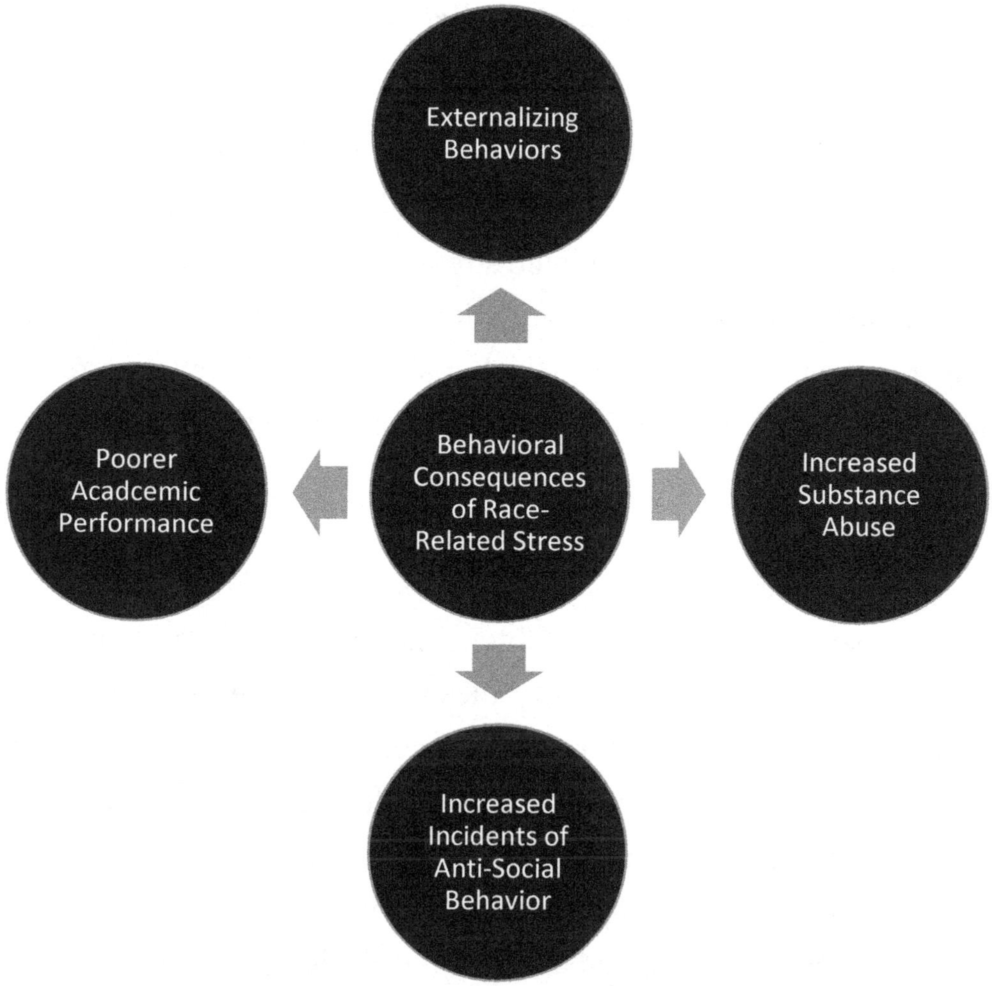

The Behavioral Consequences of Race-Related Stress

Elevated stress has been documented to have a direct relationship with adolescent behavior. Black adolescents who report being exposed to frequent instances of racism often have life issues related to externalizing behaviors. Past research has demonstrated a connection between perceived racial discrimination, substance abuse, and destructive emotional responses. Other research has found a relationship between race-related stress and antisocial behavior. Previous research has also demonstrated a relationship between race-related stress and poor academic performance in Black male youth.

Living with Race-Related Stress

At a very young age Black boys perceive themselves to be potential victims of an overpowering racist American system. These overwhelming perceptions result in the production of detrimental levels of race-related stress. These distressing amounts of race-related stress negatively impact the psychological and physiological functioning of Black male youth. The challenges of existing in such a reality are tremendously debilitating and wanting of escape.

How does a young mind escape such an engulfing situation tha is seemingly unchangeable, uncontrollable, and in the adolescent perception, eternally inescapable? How does a young mind that is already pressured by the complicated and mysterious stage of adolescence manage the psychological pain connected to fatalistic perceptions and anticipations of being treated unfairly because of his physical appearance? To investigate this question, social scientists were called upon by the Basic Behavioral Science Task Force of the National Advisory Mental Health Council to identify and examine the various behaviors utilized by individuals whose daily lives are confronted and disrupted by the intrusive forces of racism. These scholars have determined that race-related stress responses are directly related to an individual's utilization of self-protecting coping behaviors. These behaviors or "coping mechanisms", serve as an individual's means for suppressing feelings of stress that are directly related to being immersed in a social structure overrun with injustice and inequality.

Coping with Race-Related Stress

With racism, stigma, and discrimination comes the reality of various social threats to a Black male's livelihood and well-being. It is reasonable to assume that Black males experience elevated stress and other uncomfortable emotions as a result of racism, stigma, and discrimination. Coping mechanisms have been defined as "efforts to regulate emotion, cognition, behavior, physiology, and the environment in response to stressful events and circumstances". In short, when a person is "coping" they are trying to deal with or manage the stress that comes with feeling vulnerable or threatened. Numerous studies have investigated the type of coping behaviors utilized by individuals to psychologically manage hostile reactions from other members of society. These coping behaviors can be productive and empowering or counterproductive and disempowering. Put another way they can enhance psychological functioning or deteriorate psychological functioning.

The Process of Implementing a Coping Behavior

When encountering stressful situations, a two-tier process of appraisal takes place. The first level, called "primary appraisal," is when an individual examines a stressful situation to determine the impact the stressful encounter will have on their life and well-being. The second level of appraisal, called "secondary appraisal," is when an individual examines the stressful situation to determine and explore potential options and resources available for dealing with the perceptually harmful situation. Research has found that when an individual encounters stressful situations that he feels are controllable and/or changeable, he will utilize Solution-Focused Coping behaviors. In contrast, individuals confronted with situations that appear to be unchangeable or uncontrollable will typically utilize Avoidant-Focused and/or Emotion-Focused Coping behaviors.

Solution-Focused Coping

Past research has distinguished between adaptive (good) and maladaptive (bad) coping behaviors. As the result of such research, Solution-Focused Coping behaviors have been discovered to be related to positive life and psychological outcomes. Solution-Focused Coping has the primary goal of modifying or eliminating the root cause of an individual's stress. In the face of life stress, the individual utilizing Solution-Focused Coping psychologically postures himself to eliminate or alter the stress producing situation.

Solution-Focused Coping is most effective when an individual is facing a problem he actually has the power to solve (e.g. stress caused by poor money management). In contrast, Solution-Focused Coping is not as effective when an individual is facing a life-stressor in which he has no personal power to eliminate or alter (e.g. stress caused by the death of a loved one). Racism, by most people's standards, is considered to be out of any particular individual's control as the individual essentially does not have control over society's propensity to be driven by the energies of racism. In conclusion, Solution-Focused Coping alone may not be an effective strategy for coping with the stress of racism, stigma, and discrimination as essentially a Black male has little or no control over society's racist views and practices.

Avoidant-Focused Coping

Avoidant-Focused Coping behaviors have been discovered to be related to negative youth outcomes. Avoidant-Focused Coping is the practice of mentally and physically avoiding or ignoring the reality of a given stressor in one's life. This type of coping includes the individual not making any personal attempts to eliminate or alter the experienced stressor. Previous research on coping behaviors has found that low income Black males utilize Avoidant-Focused Coping behaviors as a way of dealing with stress. Researchers have identified Avoidant-Focused Coping as a type of coping that can manifest itself through withdrawal, escape, and denial.

The primary objective of Avoidant-Focused Coping (a type of disengagement coping) is the regulation or management of negative emotions caused by life-stressors. Avoidant-Focused Coping behaviors have been found to be positively correlated with depression, anxiety, conduct disorder, and maladjustment. Past research has shown that individuals who anticipate devaluation and discrimination, often utilize dysfunctional coping behaviors such as withdrawal. Such withdrawal coping is used as a means of regulating or managing the stress accompanied with these perceptions.

Researchers theorize that the use of such maladaptive coping behaviors may exacerbate the effects of life-stressors. Finally, individuals who implement maladaptive coping behaviors as a means of managing their internal and external realities often report decreased levels of life satisfaction. In conclusion, Black males who utilize Avoidant-Focused Coping as a strategy for dealing with racism, stigma, and discrimination are more likely to experience deteriorated psychological functioning, which will in turn lead to poor social functioning and poor life outcomes.

Emotion-Focused Coping

According to social scientists, individuals utilize Emotion-Focused Coping for the purposes of alleviating the undesired emotional discomfort that results from stress. Emotion-Focused Coping often expresses itself through the venting of emotions, blaming of self, accepting of responsibility for the stressor, and seeking support from others. Individuals who utilize Emotion-Focused Coping have been found to be self-preoccupied and tense. They are also more likely to blame themselves for being overemotional and are often angry. Emotional Coping has also been discovered by researchers to facilitate negative self-talk and depression. In conclusion, Black males who use Emotion-Focused Coping as a strategy for dealing with racism, stigma, and discrimination are more likely to experience deteriorated psychological functioning. This in turn will lead to poor social functioning and poor life outcomes.

Summary of Available Coping Strategies

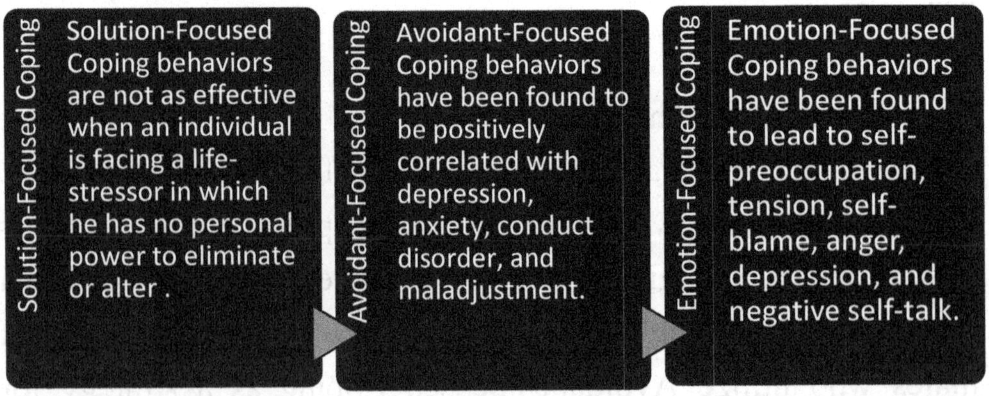

So Where are We Now?

You may have noticed that there are essentially no effective means for a Black male to cope with racism, stigma, and discrimination. Why do I say this?

Racism, stigma, and discrimination are out of the control and power of any Black male. Therefore, the use of Solution-Focused Coping alone will be ineffective as this form of coping calls for the individual to eliminate or alter the stressful situation. A Black male's attempt to eliminate racism will be like throwing a cup a water on a forest fire. Taking on the impossible task of eliminating racism will ultimately lead to deep-seated frustration which will ultimately lead to anger, depression, and anxiety. The use of Avoidant-Coping which includes behaviors such as withdrawal and escapism, will only place a Black male in a cycle of poor social performance and poor psychological functioning. The use of Emotion-Focused Coping compels a Black male to utilize behaviors such as emotional venting, self-preoccupation, and negative self-talk to deal with racism, discrimination, and stigma. Emotion-Focused Coping, just like Avoidant-Focused Coping, will ultimately lead to a cycle of poor psychological functioning which will lead to poor social functioning that will result in even poorer psychological functioning. This downward spiraling cycle of poor psychological functioning leading to poor social functioning, will continue until a poor life outcome is achieved.

In the upcoming chapter of this book I will outline a race-based coping model that merges three different coping approaches into one race-appropriate framework. This framework can be used by counselors as a tool for building productive coping skills into the minds of Black males. This form of coping is called Stigma-Focused Coping. This Stigma-Focused coping is built into the Black male psyche via the therapeutic model called Stigma Internalization Therapy (SIT). This model will be discussed in the upcoming chapter.

The Failure Schema

As previously mentioned, developing Black boys lack an effective psychological defense system as it relates to protecting themselves from the internalization of a stigmatic messaging system. As a result, Black male youth often succumb to stigma internalization and as a result develop the symptoms of an individual guided by a “failure schema”. A failure schema is built upon a combination of psychological tendencies and personality traits that make an individual predisposed to failure. Individuals with these psychological tendencies or personality traits engage in a cyclical pattern of fear, frustration, self-sabotage, withdrawal, and escapism.

The purpose of these behavior patterns in Black males is to escape from the internal stress and pressure related to living in a world that “rejects and limits you because of the color of your skin”. Thus, an addictive failure response pattern emerges as a result of the ability for the escaping behavior to provide a form of alleviation from the uncomfortable emotions that accompany stigmatic thoughts and cognition (the fear of failure, anticipated race-related catastrophe, chronic race-related pessimism, recurring sense of race-related detachment from success, etc.). The collective maladaptive coping behaviors of individual Black males functioning with a failure schema comes together to create what I have coined “*CAN’T Culture*”. This concept will be further discussed in the next few paragraphs.

What is a Failure Schema?

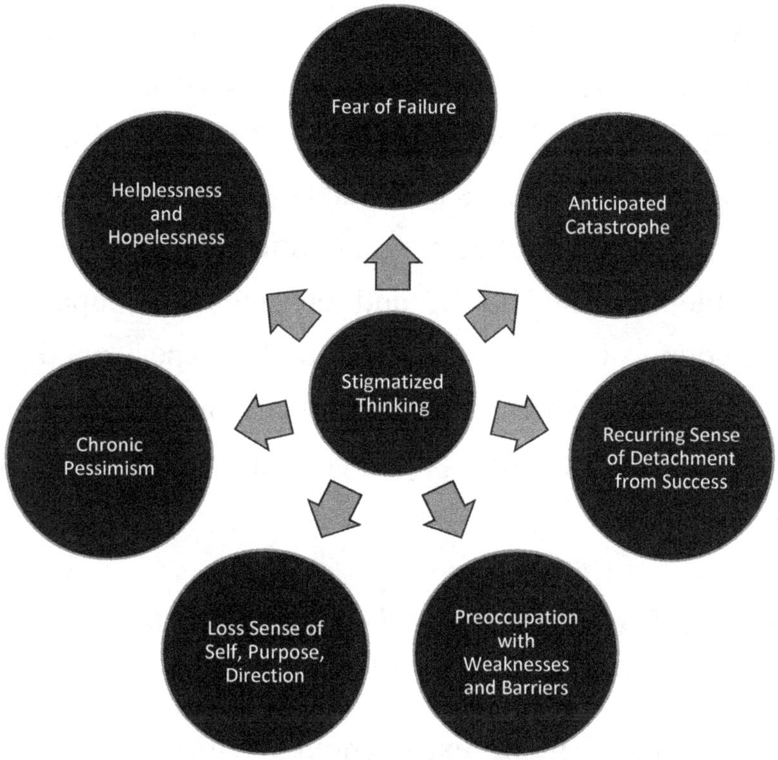

The Great Escape

Earlier in this chapter I presented the theory that race-related stress results from environmental threats to personal progress, equality, and the ability to accumulate resources. Branching from that theory, it can be assumed that Black males, in an attempt to decrease race-related stress, disengage themselves from the predetermined "American Way" of accomplishing the "American Dream". It can be assumed that at some point the Black male consciously and/or subconsciously decides that if he does not fully invest in being successful, he will not have anything to lose, which will in turn minimize his race-related stress (i.e. nothing to lose = less race-related stress; something to lose = more race-related stress).

To be confronted during the boyhood years with the reality that what you work for can be taken away and what you deserve can be withheld because of how you look is a devastating psychological blow. The consuming reality of being in a social position that makes one vulnerable to discrimination is psychologically draining. As previously asked, how does a young mind escape such an engulfing situation which is seemingly unchangeable, uncontrollable, and eternally inescapable? How does a young under-developed, under-experienced, under-resourced, and under-affirmed mind, wandering through the maze of adolescence, manage the psychological task of overcoming a racist world?

A Need for Escape Drives and Guides Maladaptive Coping Behaviors

As a Black male experiencing national rejection and national alienation, his cognitive perceptions, filters, and interpretations are going to be driven and guided by the spirit of hopelessness, shame, inferiority, guilt, and lack. As a result of his identity being forged in the fires of rejection and stigma, his worldview and self-system will be built upon the organizing principles of vulnerability, incompetence, and doubt. As a result of being raised, nurtured, and incubated in a racially-hazardous environment, Black males at a very young age methodically prepare themselves for failure. Tragically, as previously stated, many Black boys have consciously and subconsciously given themselves permission to fail. This anticipation of failure produces race-related stress, which leads to the conscious and subconscious use of coping behaviors that are not productive and will ultimately lead him down the path of underachievement.

Maladaptive Attempts to Reduce Race-Related Stress (Actions)

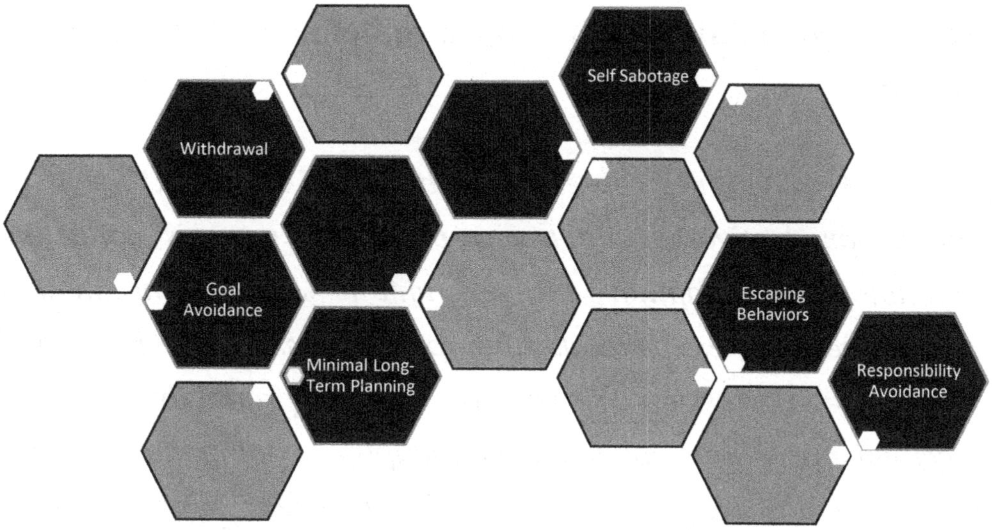

Collective Maladaptive Coping = **CAN'T** *Culture*

Cognitive and Affective Negativity Template (**CAN'T**)

What is *CAN'T Culture*? All cultures are created and sustained by ideas. CAN'T Culture is built around the collective Black male's idea that "we have little worth", "the world is unfair to us", and "we have no control over our future". Common sense tells us that dysfunctional environments by nature produce dysfunctional thinking, feeling, and behaving. CAN'T Culture is the Black male form of collective coping (sum total of individual attempts to cope with race-related stress) that sustains itself through social stigmatization, personal internalization, and maladaptive coping behaviors. CAN'T Culture expresses itself through goal avoidance, withdrawal, self-sabotage, minimal long-term planning, and the avoidance of responsibility. These behaviors serve the psychological purpose of reducing race-related stress.

The official definition I developed to define *CAN'T Culture* is below:

CAN'T Culture represents habitual or ritualized forms of counter-productive coping that represent a group's collective psychological adaption to an unfair and/or threatening environment. These maladaptive perceptions, behaviors, and forms of expression serve as counter-productive coping mechanisms. These collective maladaptive coping mechanisms serve the collective purpose of minimizing the fear, stress, sadness, anger, and frustration connected to the frequent and intense experiencing of extreme social stigma and marginalization.

These negative emotional experiences are minimized through the stigmatized group's creation of a set of norms, customs, values, and beliefs that are different from the norms, customs, values, and beliefs of the discriminating mainstream group. The stigma-constructed way of life now serves as a sub-culture or society where power and status can be attained and the complete loss of hope, pride, and esteem can be avoided. This avoidance of a complete loss of dignity, value, and self-respect is possible as an individual now has the ability to align his belief-system, self-system, and value-system to the norms, values, customs, and beliefs with the limiting and underachievement producing social norms of CAN'T *Culture.*

In conclusion to CAN'T Culture, the collective survival responses, coping strategies, defense mechanisms, and means of escape utilized by the Black male population have become a part of the collective Black male personality and culture of dysfunction. This collective culture and personality ultimately serve as internal barriers to forward progress and upward social mobility for all Black males who are a part of CAN'T Culture. This is due to the fact that these Black males have internalized a mind state that inhibits them from fully participating in the American social, political, and economic system.

Black males who are psychologically immersed in the beliefs, norms, customs, and expressions of CAN'T Culture, are role models for each other as the inform, instruct, and inspire one another with distorted messages, failure-laced expectations, and dysfunctional forms of coping and self-expression. Guided by the beliefs, expectations, and norms of CAN'T Culture, young Black males are eventually driven to obtain inferior identities that are characterized by socially inappropriate forms of expression.

Once these negative social roles are coded into the personality and character of a young Black male, these young minds begin to consciously and subconsciously pursue socially inappropriate goals that are irrelevant and ineffective as it pertains to acquiring the American Dream. This leads to a developing Black boy investing his mental and emotional energy in the goals and aspirations, of a counterculture that psychologically embraces failure and underachievement. This state of existence, if prolonged, negatively influences general decision-making and other specific areas of executive functioning (i.e. long-term planning, impulse control, emotion regulation, etc.). The reinforcing relationship between bad decision-making and stigmatism, produce deeper cognitive distortions that result in limited levels of psychological empowerment and social advancement.

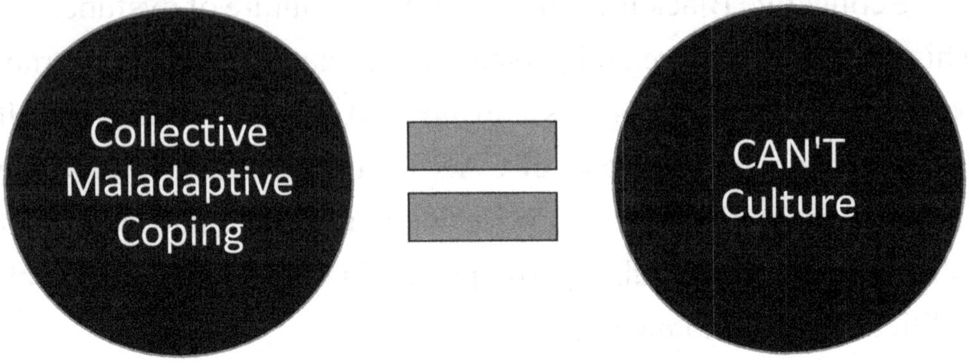

Cognitive and Affective Negativity Template (CAN'T)
(I and We – Me and Us)

CAN'T *Culture Belief-System*

Anticipated inequality and the belief that the traditional path to success is not an option (e.g. "It seems like life and the world make it impossible for people like me to achieve the American Dream.")

CAN'T *Culture Self-System*

Low self-efficacy and low self-esteem (e.g. "I have no power and I have little value in this country. Something must be wrong with me.")

CAN'T *Culture Value-System*

Alternative means for esteem and success leads to the creation of a socially ineffective value system which leads to misguided motivations (e.g. "Man I ain't going to college. What matters to me is that I ride or die for my set and my hood. The way you get respect is by having the baddest bitches, rocking the hottest gear, and driving the flyest whips.")

CAN'T *Culture Coping*

A form of psychological coping used by Black males to minimize the emotional stress and strain that comes as a result of experiencing intense national rejection (e.g. Self-Sabotage: habitually creating problems that will serve as an excuse to escape responsibility).

CAN'T *Culture Self-Efficacy*

Misguided motivation serves the purpose of finding power and control in socially ineffective aspirations in an attempt to re-secure a sense of social power and thus decrease the emotional discomfort connected to social stigma and rejection (e.g. "school is a waste of time. It is all about getting money, power, and respect in these streets.")

CAN'T *Culture Self-Image*

Built around and maintained by engaging in glamorized dysfunctional behaviors (e.g. gang affiliation meets the natural need for approval that society does not provide).

CAN'T *Culture Self-Esteem*

Comes from the ability to engage in the stereotypical and socially ineffective thinking patterns and behaviors of CAN'T Culture. These behaviors are subsituted for more socially effective or mainstream methods of attaining worth and upward social mobility (e.g. strategic attempts to gain worth and a sense of value by expressing socially inappropriate behaviors such as thugalized machismo, gang affiliation, drug dealing, etc.).

The Psychological Evolution of CAN'T *Culture*

Social engineering, cultural conditioning, and racial coding drive and guide the psychological development of Black males. To understand the causes of the current psychological functioning of Black male culture, one must critically evaluate the evolution of the Black male mind. When I say the Black male mind, I mean the collective Black male psyche, personality, and state of psychological functioning. The collective Black experience is equal to the sum total of individual Black male experiences. If you put these individual experiences together, you would get the theme or life script of the average Black male. Black male culture represents a pattern of employing similar psychological responses to similar experiences of racial oppression.

Due to the unrelenting nature of racial oppression, Black males are often situated in environments where intense barrages of racially-driven turmoil are the norm. Generations of evolving in a psychologically taxing society has resulted in the production or social engineering of a disempowered and underachieving class of American citizen. Repetitive patterns of racially-driven social traumas intensify the life issues and dramas at both the individual and collective level.

National Stigma is a term I use to describe, define, and conceptualize the reciprocal process of a nation's consistent and relentless inferiorizing of another race (deliberately and indeliberately, covertly and overtly) due to their physical characteristics. In a reciprocal process, the inferiorized racial group (deliberately and indeliberately, consciously and subconsciously) internalizes and acts out the inferiorizing messages with which they are bombarded.

Events Create History…History Creates Ideas… Ideas Create Culture

Black history represents that sequential order of social events that have guided the psychological trajectory of Black male consciousness. Black male consciousness can be defined as how Black males think and feel about their role and existence in America (their collective relationship with the rest of America). This consciousness is a collective template for surviving, responding, and coping with a racially-oppressive environment. The collective Black male consciousness and worldview represents the collective Black male identity and psyche. This Black consciousness is the collective perception, emotion, attitude, and behavioral response to the cultural abuse they have endured for several centuries.

This collective system of thinking, feeling and behaving, at one point or another, became CAN'T Culture. The cultural programming of CAN'T Culture itself is now self-sustaining. Like any established system, CAN'T Culture in an automatic fashion, passes down to future generations, the counterproductive coding, information, and instructions that were birthed out of the previous generations' stigma-driven system of thinking, feeling, and behaving. This generationally disseminated knowledge base and skill-set for survival, in all of its dysfunctionality, drives and guides the present phenomenon of Black male underachievement.

To be a perpetual victim of racial stigma is to have your cultural traditions, physical characteristics, intellectual abilities, and dialectic expressions inferiorized. It is to be universally branded to such a degree of negativity that your presence or the thought of those like you automatically generates negative perceptions and responses from the masses. The stigmatized socialization of a collective race leads to a collective psyche riddled with stigma-induced cognitions. The current collective Black male personality expresses itself in a manner that is reasonable for a group raised by previous generations of Black males who were insidiously and grossly stigmatized.

The stigmatization of the Black male has been so sustaining that today; the collective Black male image brings about a seemingly natural and automatic repulsion. In the minds of the American masses, the stigmatized Black male has now become the symbolic construct or modern day archetype for aggression, ignorance, and inferiority. Consequently, the Black male image stirs up negatives perceptions, attitudes, emotions, and behavioral responses in the majority of American citizens.

Collectively, Black males constantly experience varying forms of social discrimination. Sustained discrimination leads to social disadvantage. Sustained social disadvantage leads to disempowerment. Disempowerment leads to a loss of drive, value, and direction which leads to disorganization and dysfunction. This system of disorganization and dysfunction becomes culture. The resulting culture then becomes the psychological curriculum used for programming the future generations of Black males.

In the end, the next generation of Black males will continue to reinforce the collective psychological functioning of CAN'T Culture. Ultimately, they will as did the generation before them, pass down the collective psychological norms and practices of CAN'T Culture, to the next generation of Black males. As a result we have the multigenerational transmission of dysfunction and disorganization.

Collective Developmental Experiences = Collective Functioning

Ideas, information, and experiences are the gears of any system of conditioning. In order for any system of conditioning to be effective it has to be structured, systematic, and programmatic in nature. It has to be a type of social curriculum for educating the masses. The ideas, information, and experiences given to Black males are rooted in racism, stigma, and discrimination. These conditioning variables produce psychological experiences of hopelessness, fear, frustration, sadness, and anxiety. These resulting emotions trigger escaping behaviors which produce social underachievement.

CAN'T Culture Chain of Logic: Collective Victimhood, Collective Entitlement, and Collective System Dependence

The collective psychological functioning of the Black male represents how Black males mentally perceive and interpret information from reality. It is a stigma-founded framework for psychologically organizing and cataloging the data of life. What is the collective psyche of the Black male? The current state of the collective Black male's level of psychological functioning is a reflection of stigma-internalization. The current social plight of the Black male is the outward manifestation of disorganized and dysfunctional attempts to psychologically cope with racism, stigma, and discrimination. The primary dysfunctional and disorganized ways in which Black males cope with racism are driven by stigmatic chains of logic. The three primary links that hold together this chain of logic are a cycle of collective victimhood, a collective sense of entitlement, and collective system dependence.

The entitlement coping response occurs when a Black male believes that since Black males have been generationally marginalized, they are morally owed something from a system that has continually withheld deserved social resources and opportunities. They feel in general, that America is indebted to them and therefore America should give them everything they need to construct their American Dream. In essence, they are saying, "because of what the system has done to Black people in the past, life is harder for me today and therefore it is the responsibility of the same system to improve my current conditions".

Black males who utilize this type of coping invest minimal amounts of energy, time, and effort towards long-term planning and personal responsibility. Black males who utilize this approach to living often wait for others to provide them the resources or tools they need to be successful. By not investing much personal time and energy into achieving the American Dream, these Black males experience decreased race-related stress as they have less self-investment (i.e. less self-investment = less to lose = less risk = less race-related stress = less psychological battles with the fear of failure). The assumption is "if someone gives it to me, I will not have to worry so much about someone taking what I have earned or withholding what I rightfully deserve".

This type of collective learned helplessness is a result of shared oppression, shared vulnerability, and a shared inability to defend the individual and collective self from marginalization and oppression. This shared victimhood, alongside collective memories of stigma and discrimination, has disempowered many Black males to the point that their overwhelming sense of powerlessness produces self-limiting perspectives, which ultimately leads to system-dependence. System-dependence is a type of maladaptive coping in that it serves the purpose of stress reduction. In essence, system-dependence is the act of only acquiring what the system will allow you to have as a trade-off for dealing with the stress connected to the fear of having your deserved resources withheld or taken away.

Individuals who have such a strong sense of powerlessness are difficult to recondition because they naturally block out information that signals the potential for power and progress. Oftentimes, these individuals have a restricted ability to respond to empowering information, people, and experiences. These individuals usually psychologically channel information in a way that secures mental and emotional comfort even if it means psychologically accepting a life of system-funded poverty. This blueprint for failure is further reinforced by national stigma and rejection. Until Black males are trained and conditioned to effectively respond to racism, stigma, and discrimination, this devastating cycle will only intensify.

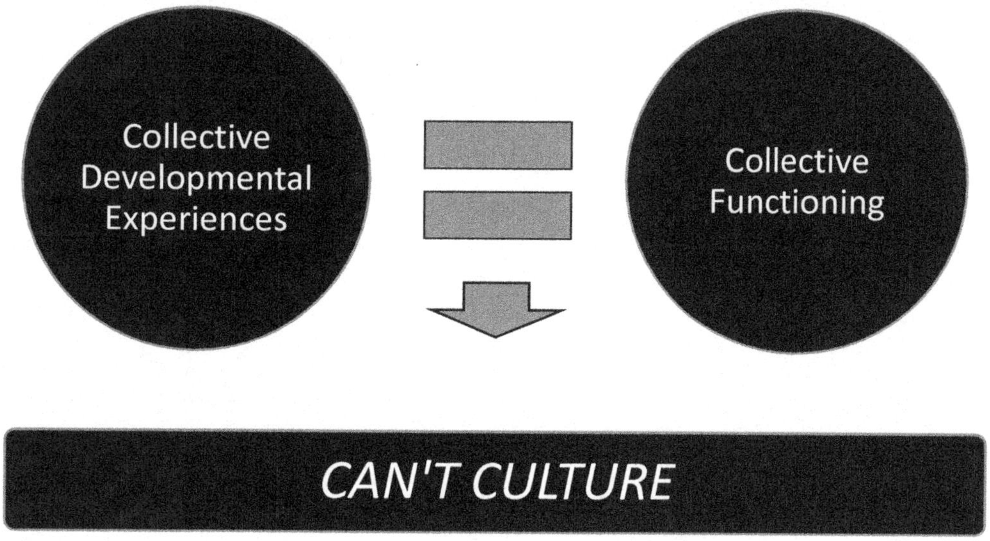

SECTION III.

RECONDITIONING SOULS: THE ART AND SCIENCE OF COUNSELING BLACK MALES

The Psychology of Racism 3

Reconditioning Souls: The Art and Science of Counseling Black Males

Stigma Psychology: A Systematic Theory-Based Explanation for Black Male Thought and Behavior

History has taught Black males that they have limited opportunities, access, resources, and potential for upward mobility. Inevitably, the root of Black male psychological functioning is linked to learning how to survive marginalization, disadvantage, and poverty. The lessons of history have educated Black men to see themselves as powerless and vulnerable. As a sad result, Black males examine their American reality through the lens of threat. This lens guides how Black males collectively interpret, define, and give meaning to their collective American experience.

Black males have similar psychological functioning because they have similar psychological experiences that are rooted in shared social experiences. These shared experiences and struggles have birthed their collective interests, strengths, values, habits, goals, weaknesses, challenges, etc. These collective traits make up the culture of the masculine member of arguably the youngest race on the planet (i.e. 500 years ago Black Americans did not exist). Individual Black male self-efficacy and self-esteem is connected to the collective Black male's sense of self-efficacy and self-esteem. As a culture, Black males feel they have failed to overcome their social barriers. Consequently, the Black male's collective levels of self-efficacy are insufficient as it relates to being equipped with the internal energies necessary to pursue the American Dream. The Black male's collective frame of reference and state of mind as it relates to the American Dream is contained in a box of fear and insufficiency.

The collective identity of the Black male represents the sum total of their past, present, and expected future experiences with American racism, stigma, and discrimination. As a result of transgenerational racism, stigma, and discrimination, the collective Black male's culture, identity, worldview, and self-system is built upon the organizing principles of inferiority, vulnerability, and lack. The terrible result is a life-view crippled by perceptions and assumptions of having little control over their lives.

Psychological Warfare

America's race-driven processes and procedures have imposed insidious forms of psychological warfare (the threat of being placed in a mental, emotional, and/or physical state in which suffering will take place) on the Black male species on a moment-to-moment, day-to-day, and century-to-century basis. The psychological stress and strain of American racism has caused the ultimate goal and driving force of Black male decision-making to be the accomplishing of pain alleviation (mental and/or emotional). American racism has relentlessly placed Black males in exploitative positions that trigger mental and emotional weaknesses as well as stir up dysfunctional behavior.

The overall theory presented in this book identifies social stigmatization and maladaptive coping strategies as the specific mediators connecting Black males to academic and social underachievement. It appears that Black males are in a position in which they are faced with extreme levels of race-related stress. However, due to the unavoidable and inevitable nature of racism, Solution-Focused Coping is not a viable option and in like manner, Avoidant-Focused and Emotion-Focused Coping only lead to deeper levels of psychological dysfunction.

It can thus be theorized that collectively, Black males are psychologically ill-equipped to effectively cope with the stresses of systemic stigmatization. This lack of a psychological defense system in the face of American racism has resulted in generations of psychologically defenseless and vulnerable Black boys evolving into psychologically defenseless and vulnerable Black men. In a twisted essence, Black males are placed in the following dooming situation:

a. *In the face of racism, a Black male can utilize a Solution-Focused form of coping that will only lead to disempowering levels of frustration, sadness, and/or anger.*

b. *In the face of racism, a Black male can utilize Avoidant-Focused and/or Emotion-Focused forms of coping that ultimately leads to frustration, sadness and/or anger.*

Psychological Warfare

These two options both seem to lead a Black boy down a path of certain sociological and psychological doom. In order to help bring a solution to this cruel psychosocial scenario, I have developed an integrated coping approach for building psychological resilience into Black males. This internal "Spirit of Resilience" is critical and necessary in order to reverse the negative impact of racism on the psychological functioning of Black males.

Stigma-Suppression Coping (SSC)
A 3-Dimensional Approach for Effectively Responding to Racism, Stigma, and Discrimination

The Stigma-Suppression Coping approach merges Solution-Focused Coping, Appraisal Focused Coping, and Emotion-Focused Coping. I have found a combination of these three coping approaches to be very beneficial when providing therapy to Black male clients who exhibit signs of stigma internalization.

In this model:

1. *Solution-Focused Coping* focuses on minimizing a client's potential for internalizing negative stigmatic messages and experiences. This form of coping focuses on the specific steps, actions, and strategies a Black male can use to deal with the stress resulting from racism, stigma, and discrimination. The overall strategy has the ultimate purpose of making certain that the Black male does not internalize society's negative messages about his personhood. As it relates to stigma suppressing Solution-Focused Coping, the problem to be solved is not ending, controlling, or avoiding

racism. The problem to be solved is to un-internalize or not internalize stigma. Furthermore, the problem is not changing racism, in contrast, it is not letting racism change you.

2. *Appraisal-Focused Coping* focuses on the processing, filtering, and interpretation approaches a Black male can use to deal with the stress resulting from racism, stigma, and discrimination. This form of coping focuses on processing experiences of racism, stigma, and discrimination in a way that actually empowers the Black male to not accept, identify with, or internalize society's negative messages about his personhood. As it relates to stigma suppressing Appraisal-Focused Coping, stigma and racism are appraised as deliberate attempts to sabotage the life, liberty, and legacy of the Black male. This personification of the spirit of racism makes racism a more tangible enemy. The dark agenda of racism now can serve as a means of increasing a Black male's sense of duty and responsibility to un-internalize or avoid internalizing racial stigma. With this system of appraisal, stigma and racism are processed, filtered, and interpreted in a manner that fosters a sense of power, hope, and empowerment.

3. *Emotion-Focused Coping* focuses on effective strategies for emotion management that a Black male can use to deal with the stress that results from racism, stigma, and discrimination. This form of coping focuses on identifying productive ways of alleviating, expressing, and channeling emotions. The methods of emotional expression utilized by the Black male must be in some way connected to the overall goal of not internalizing society's negative messages about

his personhood. As it relates to stigma suppressing Emotion-Focused Coping, the Black male makes a strategic effort to not express his emotions in the maladaptive and stereotypical ways in which he was trained and conditioned.

Stigma-Suppressing Coping (SSC) via Stigma Internalization Therapy (SIT)

This 3-dimensional style of stigma-suppressing coping effectively empowers the Black male to not let his experiences with racism trigger dysfunctional thoughts, emotions, and behaviors. This 3-dimensional stigma-appropriate form of coping empowers a Black male client to control his perceptual responses, his emotional responses, and his behavioral responses to racism. Such productive coping will minimize the ability of racism to negatively affect a Black male's relationships and general social performance. In this 3-dimensional style of coping, a Black male is in fact controlling how he thinks about his stigmatizing experiences, how he expresses the emotions connected to his stigmatizing experiences, and what behaviors he will use to overcome his stigmatic experiences. This 3-dimensional system of coping, when used effectively and routinely in a supportive environment will result in decreased levels of psychological stress as the Black male client will begin to, and continue to, realize the power he has to un-internalize or avoid the internalization of National Stigma. This system of Stigma-Suppression Coping is built into the Black male client via a therapist's utilization of Stigma Internalization Therapy (SIT).

Psychological Architecture: Using Stigma Internalization Therapy (SIT) as a Blueprint for Empowerment

The agenda of American racism, stigma, and discrimination is to induce the breakdown of logical, strategic, deliberate, and long-term thinking on the part of Black males. This breakdown or degeneration of appropriate reasoning takes place at a steady and sequential rate. Thus, the science of Stigma Internalization Therapy (SIT) seeks to reverse the negative effects of racism, stigmatization, and discrimination on the psychological functioning of Black males. What is SIT? SIT is a strategic therapeutic intervention that is contextualized around the psychosocial experiences of Black males. SIT was designed to empower therapists with the tools necessary to empower their Black male clients.

When working with Black males, SIT should be used as a tool to assist clients in correcting racially-constructed misperceptions that hinder their attempts to strategize and achieve a consistent pattern of productive decision-making. The SIT approach to therapy is structured to assist a therapist in the process of isolating and examining each component of the Black male client's psychological system. This isolation and examination is done with the specific purpose of diagnosing, treating, and reassembling the Black male client's mental, emotional, and behavioral system. This sequential and methodical reassembling is carried out in a fashion that fosters improved psychological and social functioning.

Using SIT as a microscope, a therapist must make a deliberate effort to identify and examine the racially-driven maladaptive behavior styles their Black male client may be utilizing in his attempts to navigate the internal and external challenges he may encounter in his interactions with his environment. The SIT approach has the strategic focus and goal of challenging and correcting stigma-induced perceptual processes that trigger counterproductive behavior patterns.

Reverse Engineering the Psychological System

The SIT intervention to assessing and improving the psychological functioning of Black males is always systematic but not always sequential. The sequence of the SIT guided questioning approach is not the overarching or essential aspect of the SIT process. What is essential for the therapist practicing SIT is that at some point, each component of the person's psychological system is isolated, examined, diagnosed, treated, and put back together in a manner that fosters optimal psychological functioning.

SIT should be viewed as a therapeutic manual for engaging in a technical process of therapy, which mirrors the process of reverse engineering. In this process, SIT purposely engages the therapist in the systematic process of separating and isolating the cognitive components (mental, emotional, and behavioral) of the client's psychological functioning. This process is performed in a focused effort to isolate and analyze these individual parts. This process of isolating the aforementioned individual psychological components is done in an attempt to determine their relatedness to and dependence upon one another (i.e. how emotions affect thoughts, how thoughts affect emotions, how thoughts affect behavior, how emotions affect behavior, how behavior affects thoughts, and how behavior effects emotions).

If applied correctly, SIT effectively assists the therapist in organizing and simplifying the information gathered during therapy sessions. Ultimately, this makes the therapist more effective at discerning and assessing whether or not their Black male client's problems are stigma-induced. The chart below outlines the specific assessment goals of the SIT process.

Assessing for Stigmatic Psychological Functioning

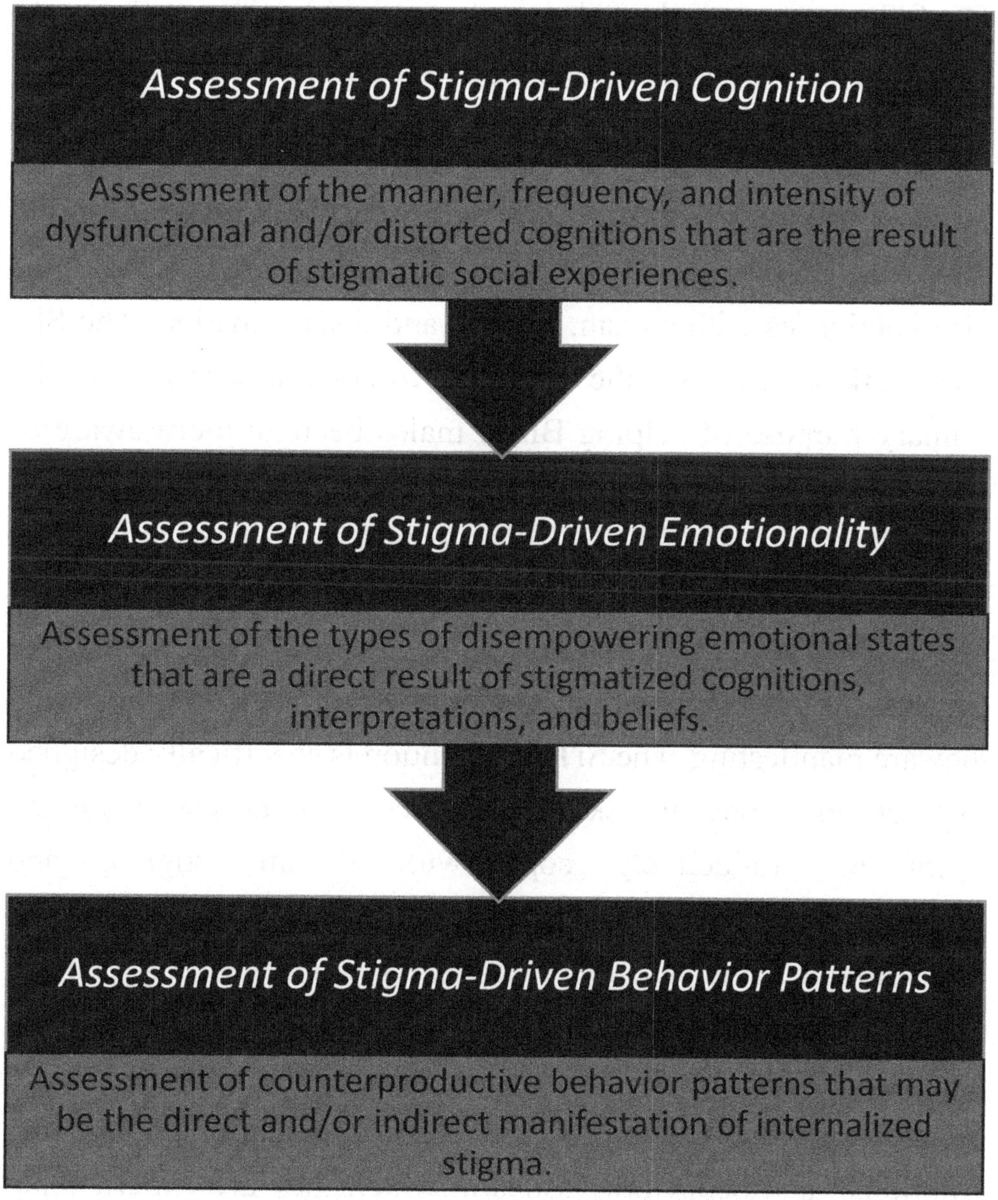

Stigmatic Cognition Interventions

The SIT philosophy assumes that Black male issues are fundamentally rooted, caused, and maintained by the experiencing and reinforcing of stigmatic messaging. The perceptual view in which Black males observe, examine, organize, and understand their life experiences is from a vantage point of powerlessness, shame, and fear of failure. As a result of this mental framework, internalized stigma causes life challenges in general to be perpetually associated with an impending sense of personal doom. The SIT approach seeks to bring about a productive resolution to unresolved issues related to and/or resulting from stigma-induced cognitive misperceptions.

A major purpose of Stigmatic Cognitive Interventions is to improve a Black male client's ability to productively psychologize his experiences with racism, stigma, and discrimination. The SIT intervention uses Stigmatic Cognitive Interventions that serve the primary purpose of helping Black males become more aware of any stigma-induced misperceptions that may be negatively impacting their lives. The SIT intervention is designed to uncover for the client, the preceding life and/or social experiences responsible for, and/or connected to the resulting destructive perceptions, disempowering emotions, and behavioral patterns they are manifesting. The SIT intervention is specifically designed to teach and model the skills and perceptions necessary for the client to productively cope with racism, stigma, and discrimination. This internalizing of a productive coping-system, will ultimately increase a Black male's chances of achieving a positive life outcome. The SIT intervention is further designed to help Black males become increasingly aware of how these stigma-induced perceptions both cause and maintain the mental, emotional, and behavioral issues in which they are experiencing and externalizing.

Stigmatic Emotional Interventions

Another major purpose of Stigmatic Emotional Interventions in SIT is to improve emotional intelligence. Improved emotional intelligence in SIT serves the purpose of empowering a Black male client to successfully handle the racially-charged emotions (e.g. depression, anxiety, loneliness, anger, etc.) that have traditionally had a negative impact on his decision-making. Furthermore, increasing emotional intelligence results in the increasing of the Black male's ability to feel, use, communicate, recognize, remember, learn from, manage, be motivated by, and understand his emotional experiences. This emotional enlightenment undoubtedly will result in the increased possibility of long-standing behavioral change.

Stigmatic Emotional Interventions are also an effective means of helping Black males bring to the surface unprocessed emotions that may be clouding their thought processes. Stigmatic Emotional Interventions can also work effectively to bring about an emotional catharsis during therapy. Such an emotional cleansing may be beneficial to Black males because of the ability of catharsis in SIT to clear out stigma-induced emotions that are not beneficial to the overall psychological functioning of the Black male client. During this process, racially-charged social experiences that arouse and energize negative emotions are reframed and given positive meaning so that memories of past stigmatizing experiences are made less effective in their ability to incite negative emotions within the Black male client. Past, present, and anticipated future experiences with racism and stigma are also discussed. In the stigmatic emotional interventions strategies and approaches for fostering effective emotional responding, coping, and adjustment are utilized during therapy sessions.

Stigmatic Behavioral Interventions

When utilized in a therapeutic setting, SIT is a systematic and scientific process in which behavior is assessed, behavior changing goals are set, and a behavior changing treatment plan is outlined. In this dimension of the SIT intervention, behavior change and therapeutic outcomes are also evaluated. Furthermore, the behavioral dimension of the SIT intervention is used to identify and assess counterproductive behaviors. In this dimension of the SIT intervention, goals for behavioral change are strategically established. These interventions work collectively as a system for producing cognitive restructuring, emotion management, and behavioral change.

In Conclusion to Stigma Internalization Therapy…

The SIT philosophy assumes that Black males present in therapy with issues (e.g. relationships, mood, behavioral, etc.) related to, or resulting from their experiences with racism, stigma, and discrimination. The SIT approach functions under the assumption that most Black male issues are dependent upon or interrelated with stigma-induced thoughts, feelings, and behaviors. The SIT intervention assumes that stigma-induced cognitions, emotions, and behaviors are learned over the life-span and thus can also be unlearned. The SIT intervention in the therapeutic setting serves as a platform for educating Black males on how to relearn productive perceptual, emotional, and behavioral responses to their past, present, and future experiences with racism, stigma, and discrimination.

The ultimate goal of SIT is the production of positive growth in the areas of cognitive restructuring, emotional intelligence, and behavior modification. As a therapist practicing SIT, you will interact with Black males who will present with issues related to stress, anxiety, depression, and other forms of mental, emotional, and behavioral concerns. Many of these issues and concerns will directly and/or indirectly relate to his racially-charged social experiences and subsequent psychological functioning. Failure to provide a Black male with an opportunity to process race-based mental, emotional, and behavioral issues may greatly complicate the ability of any therapist to assist the Black male client in effectively accomplishing his therapeutic goals.

The SIT philosophy asserts that Black males discover and understand themselves and their experiences as individuals through the context of their racial characteristics and racially-charged social experiences. The effects of racially-charged social experiences on the psychological development of the Black male mind is unceasing and life-long. Any Black male immersed in American society is psychologically affected (positively and negatively, consciously, and/or subconsciously) by these social experiences. The SIT intervention understands that a Black male's racial characteristics play a part (due to social influences) on his psychological functioning and developmental trajectory. At every stage of the Black male's human growth and development, racial characteristics, and social experiences are present and play the most pivotal of roles.

A therapist practicing SIT has the task of facilitating a therapeutic discussion that maximizes the flow of race-related information presented throughout any given session. Furthermore, a therapist utilizing SIT must effectively maximize the amount of self-awareness and life understanding attained by the Black male client. The therapist practicing SIT should maintain a climate in which perceptions, emotions, and behaviors can be understood as the ultimate causes of the Black male's current state of social existence. A therapist practicing SIT should endeavor to actively engage the client in thinking, listening, feeling, and talking at all levels of the therapeutic process while creating, maintaining, and facilitating an atmosphere in which perceptual, emotional, and behavioral change can flourish.

Merging Stigma Internalization Therapy (SIT) and the Adaptive Life Processing Model (ALP)

The Adaptive Life Processing model (ALP) is a universal therapeutic model for nurturing productive coping, effective adaption, positive reframing, and maximized life processing. As the developer of the ALP approach to therapy, I strongly affirm the appropriateness of contextualizing the ALP approach around the psychosocial experiences of Black males. (Note: The Adaptive Life Processing Model can also be contextualized to other specific populations of clients based on race, culture, gender, psychological challenges, life experiences, etc.)

The SIT guided ALP platform is a strategically contextualized model that serves the specific purpose of building resilience, adaptive coping, confidence, and hope into the minds of the highly stigmatized Black male client. This contextualized approach works to teach Black males effective approaches for perceiving, evaluating, interpreting, responding, and ultimately coping with racism, stigma, and discrimination. The SIT guided ALP platform can provide a Black male with a safe and supportive setting where he can practice newly acquired reasoning skills and coping behaviors. The SIT guided ALP intervention makes a deliberate, intentional, and strategic effort to use a strength-based approach that identifies and capitalizes on the psychological strengths and assets of Black males.

The racially-contextualized SIT guided ALP approach therapeutically captures and treats the intersection between experiences of stigma, coping behavior utilization, psychological dysfunction, and poor life outcomes. Specifically, the racially-contextualized ALP framework places a deliberate focus on identifying how the utilization of maladaptive coping negatively impacts the life trajectory of Black males. The racially-contextualized SIT guided ALP model makes an intentional effort to outline strategies that effectively instill into Black males the adaptive behaviors necessary to cope productively with the challenges of racism, stigma, and discrimination.

The SIT guided ALP model is a psychological processing model contextualized for the treatment of accumulated stigmatic experiences. Race-conscious adaptive life processing is the act of re-psychologizing racism, stigma, and discrimination in a manner in which past racialized experiences become fuel and empowerment for achieving success in America. In therapy, a client is fully engaging in Adaptive Life Processing when they are thinking with the purpose of re-thinking, re-feeling, re-framing, re-conditioning, and re-covering. The goal of the SIT guided ALP approach is to replace disempowering thoughts and teach strategies for productively coping with the uncomfortable emotions that result from experiencing race-related stress.

The SIT guided ALP model serves as a prescriptive race-based therapeutic model designed to minimize the damaging impact of racism, stigma, discrimination, and maladaptive coping on the psychological functioning of Black males. This goal is accomplished by instilling in Black males the psychological skill set and developmental assets necessary to productively cope with and process their experiences with racism (i.e. not internalizing stigmatizing and inferiorizing messages).

Reverse Engineering the Mind via the Racially-Contextualized ALP Process

Most Black male clients will present in therapy with relational, environmental, mental, and emotional issues that are deeply-seated in failed attempts to belong, resemble, and connect to American culture. These failed attempts to belong, resemble, and connect to American culture are closely connected to the thoughts, feelings, and behaviors experienced and exhibited by Black males. Each phase of the racially-contextualized ALP process has the purpose of bringing about positive change in the cognitive, emotional, and behavioral aspects of the Black male experience.

The spirit of racism represents the master gear of America's political, educational, and economic system. Generations of exploitation and marginalization have left millions of Black males demoralized and forced to exist with a weakened sense of self-efficacy, confidence, and purpose. This state of existence often leads to deficient long-term planning, negative affect, low impulse-control, and difficulties with delaying gratification. This is the default result of functioning with stigma informed beliefs, values, and self-perceptions. The cumulative effects of consistent experiences of mass social rejection create disempowering thoughts (cognitive tumors) which serve as a Black male's stigma-informed template for living, which ultimately produces personality flaws and character defects that drive dysfunctional decision-making. The goal of the SIT driven ALP process is to help Black males control their responses to intrusive memories of social rejection and ultimately live happier lives.

The goal of SIT guided ALP process is to create an internal system (problem solving, conflict resolution, decision making, emotion management, critical thinking, etc.) that can conquer the external system of racism, stigma, and discrimination. The science of the SIT driven ALP process reduces thoughts, emotions, and behaviors into parts and analyzes them individually in isolation. This isolation allows for the effective identification of how a Black male client's thoughts, emotions, and behaviors are fueling his presenting problems. Providing a Black male client with a safe space to tell his American story, via guided questioning, allows the therapist to serve as a mirror reflecting back to the client the life images he presents. This will in future sessions help the Black male client come up with the answers and levels of processing necessary to effectively find closure with the past and confidence in the future.

The chart on the following page gives a brief outline of the eight components of the Adaptive Life Processing mode (ALP).

The Eight Stages of the Adaptive Life Processing Model (ALP)

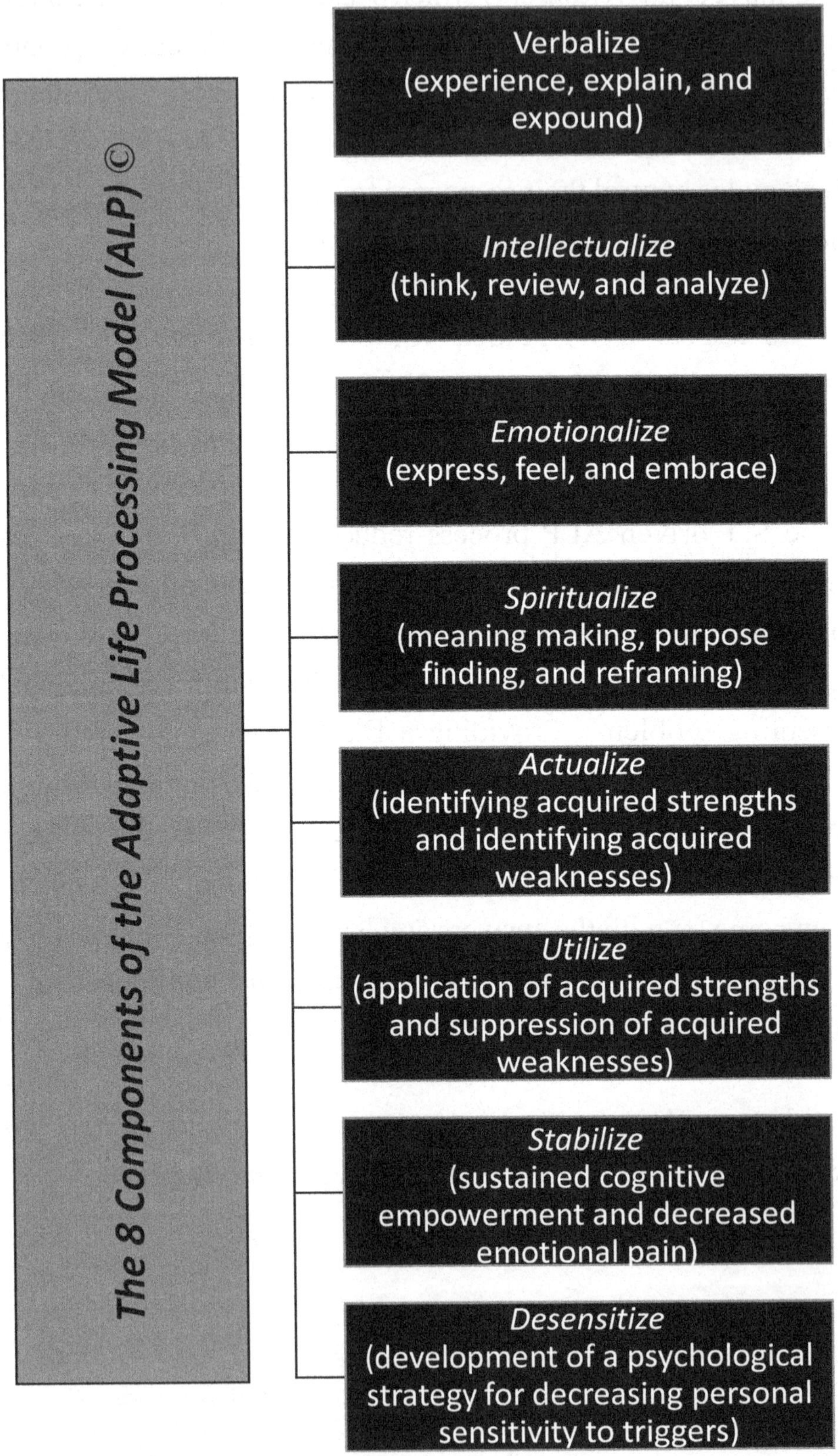

The Eight Stages of the Stigma Internalization Therapy Driven ALP: Building a Psychological Defense System

Verbalize

Reality is made up of people, places, and things. People, places and things come together to create social events. The social events we experience make up our life experiences. We have evolved psychologically according to the social experiences that make up our life history. Our social experiences serve as psyche and schema shaping mechanisms. By allowing a client an opportunity to give a descriptive account of their life experiences, memories, and interactions with the people, places, and things in their personal reality, you are helping them connect present thoughts and emotions with past experiences. By allowing a client to narrate the movie of their life, you allow them the opportunity to explain in descriptive wording how they psychologically see, touch, hear, and feel reality.

It is imperative in therapy that a Black male client has the opportunity to review problematic circumstances that may have been a direct or indirect result of his racial features. By verbalizing the list of experiences that have caused psychological discomfort and presently intrude on life satisfaction, a Black male client will increase his ability to think critically about his life experiences. Verbalization is a type of verbal journal entry that gives the client an opportunity to detail the exact nature of the life events that have caused set-back, disappointment, regret, remorse, fear, and pain. Structured verbalization opens the door to deeper levels of psychological processing.

Intellectualize

One's life story is equal to the sum total of one's social interactions. Early experiences of social neglect, rejection, and abandonment influence the personality, temperament, and disposition of Black males. Most of a Black male's presenting problems will be related to dysfunctional attempts to deal with the frustration caused by unmet socio-emotional needs. Humans are naturally driven to seek connection and a sense of belonging. Black males for half a millennium, have failed in their attempts to belong and connect to American culture. The emotional pain that results from an inability to fulfill the relational and socio-emotional drives of humankind can lead to desperation, distorted thinking, and dysfunctional behaviors.

In the SIT driven ALP process, the Intellectualization of life events means critically reflecting on the problematic social events that have negatively affected perceptions, emotions, and behaviors. Intellectualizing helps a Black male find understanding as it relates to how experiences with racism, stigma, and discrimination have led to bad decision-making and maladaptive coping. Intellectualization not only helps the Black male client find understanding but it also helps him recognize his need for healing.

The goal of Intellectualization is to critically analyze life experiences with the goal of discovering unanswered questions, challenge stigma-informed perspectives, and confront maladaptive attributions via enhanced self-awareness. Intellectualization in the SIT driven ALP process allows for the intellectual confrontation of dysfunctional interpretations, counter-productive defense mechanisms, and disempowering associations. By intellectually processing how racism, stigma, and discrimination have affected how a Black male client defines manhood, blackness, life, and his American experience, a therapist fosters the critical information needed to help the client educate himself on the impact of these experiences on his thinking, feeling, and behaving. Such enlightenment will help the Black male client gain an intellectual understanding of the consequences of these negative events. By providing the Black male client with a platform for critically analyzing his life experiences, a therapist is providing their client with a chance to develop a theory or hypothesis on why things have happened the way that they have and how these experiences have negatively impacted his life.

Emotionalize

Black males, like all males, are socialized to suppress their feelings by deliberately avoiding discussions, conversations, and interactions that elicit emotional experiences. Blocking out the emotions Black males have experienced as a result of racism is a consuming task that monopolizes energy that should be devoted to self-actualization. The purpose of Emotionalizing in the SIT driven ALP process is to give Black males the opportunity to unclog or release built-up and unprocessed emotions that relate to general life issues as well as race-related life issues. This type of emotional cleansing is restorative as it provides the Black male client an opportunity to acknowledge that life in America has been stressful, frustrating, hurtful, and sometimes enraging. This opportunity for masculine vulnerability frees the client to come to terms with the pain and begin the process of problem solving. This cleansing of unexpressed pain, fear, and disappointment allows for the purging of repressed emotions that have become detrimental to the self-actualizing process. This emptying of emotions cleanses the soul and allows for a clearer connection to cognitive restructuring.

Men are not generally comfortable expressing emotions (especially sadness and fear, anger is sometimes acceptable as it gives a false sense of power). The mass of unresolved emotions related to being engulfed in a system that violently assaults a Black male client's racial characteristics negatively impacts the thinking and behavior dimensions of his psychological system. Many Black men, as a result of "thugalized machismo", bottle their emotions or channel them towards unproductive behaviors. Emotional processing involves talking about issues with the purpose of identifying the emotional toll connected to living in a racist nation. The release of emotion by itself is ineffective in terms of psychotherapy if it does not play a productive role in cognitive restructuring. Emotionalizing should lead to enhanced thinking (aided by guided questioning and conversation) as well as be used as motivation for change and achieving closure.

Emotionalizing provides the opportunity to capture the knowledge, wisdom, and inspiration embedded in a client's feelings. It allows the opportunity to learn effective strategies for the productive emotional registering and emotional responding of stigmatizing life experiences. Although emotional catharsis may not always take the form of sadness, emotional catharsis will usually manifest itself in some form of verbal venting and/or tears. Recognizing, communicating, and expressing painful emotions that are linked to stigmatic experiences results in a type of cognitive liberation as pain is released and emotional debris is cleansed from the soul.

Spiritualize

Spiritualizing involves establishing a chosen course of logic, reasoning, and interpretation that brings purpose and meaning to life's craziness and randomness. The spiritual processing of negative life events is not about religion but about finding meaning. A therapist using the SIT driven ALP process utilizes guided questioning to incite productive reasoning that confronts irrational thinking and disempowering interpretations of racism, stigma, and discrimination. This should ultimately lead to the inception of a more positive and productive reframing of the typical Black male's life history.

In the spiritual processing phase, a client serves as a tour guide walking the therapist through their system of logic and reasoning as it relates to the negative perceptions and dysfunctional assumptions they have acquired as a result of stigmatic experiences. By discussing their stigma-driven conclusions, the therapist can work to help the client construct more purposeful, empowering, and productive conclusions about their past and present life challenges. By helping the client make sense and bring a higher purpose to the movie of their life, the therapist is helping instill a dimension of resilience that will help the Black male client overcome his personal and social challenges. Such purpose-driven processing will increase the client's sense of security and personal worth. The Spiritualization of life calls for the gradual development of a meaning-making system that protects the self-esteem and psychic energy of the Black male client. This portion of a Black male's psychological defense system will improve his capacity for meeting life's general demands while he continues to thrive in a racist society.

When spiritualizing life, a client is giving an empowering explanation to his social trials and a purpose-driven meaning to his cultural struggles. By giving deeper purpose and meaning to his American struggles, a Black male is slowly internalizing a belief system that allows him to interpret racism, stigma, and discrimination in a manner that will multiply his resiliency levels. This spiritualizing helps the client focus his attention on the potential positive outcomes of his struggles in America. This is in stark contrast to focusing only on the possible negative outcomes of his American struggle. With such an empowering messaging system resounding in his head, life situations seem a little less intimidating and this Black male client will be more capable of sustaining positive perspectives and esteem levels.

In conclusion to spiritual processing, life struggles that appear to have no rhyme or reason leads to despair and a sense of hopelessness. Replacing randomness with reason minimizes stress, despair, and the sense of victimhood. When Black males lack spiritual information (meaning) regarding their struggle, they fill these areas of lack with fear and doubt. By connecting meaning to a Black male's challenging American experiences, you are expanding and enhancing his psychological defense system.

Actualize

The resulting shame, secrets, and fears produced by social trauma govern the perceptions of Black males. These perceptions govern Black male behavior at the individual and collective level. When we think of individuals who are immersed in stigmatic environments, we think of people who eventually evolve into persons who have a propensity to utilize a specific set of dysfunctional behaviors. We assume that this person's eventual outcome will be the by-product of their environmentally acquired weaknesses, personality flaws, and character defects. In the Actualizing stage of the SIT Driven ALP approach, the focus is turned away from the negative psychological attributes that a Black male may acquire as a result of being indoctrinated by stigmatizing cultural conditioning. In a dramatically different twist for counseling Black males, the focus of therapy is to identify the acquired talents, strengths, and abilities these struggles have built into their personhood.

Achieving Actualization requires mental, emotional, and spiritual empowerment. The goal of the Actualizing phase of the SIT driven ALP approach is similar to every other phase in the ALP process - *holistic processing that leads to personal empowerment*. The ALP model defines closure as "closing the door" on the ability of the past to negatively impact the present and the future. The goal of the Actualizing phase is for the Black male to discover the strengths, assets, and skill set for living he has developed as a result of his trials with stigma. Increased focus on acquired strengths result in the stigmatized Black male identifying and ultimately utilizing the mental, emotional, and spiritual strengths he has acquired as a result of his American struggles. The Actualization phase furthermore assists clients in strategically transporting and superimposing their psychological strengths over their general life challenges. During the Actualizing phase, a therapist should make an intentional effort to help the client practice newly acquired life skills that will help him overcome his exterior barriers. These life skills include problem-solving, conflict-resolution, assertiveness, effective communication, critical thinking, decision-making, and emotion management.

Utilize

The purpose of the Utilization phase of the SIT guided ALP intervention is to psychologically "un-handicap" Black males so that they keep pace in the Information Age. Black males have to "dig deep" within themselves to discover both the raw talent and abilities they are blessed with, as well as the talents and abilities they have acquired as a result of struggle. This strategy for building resilience involves teaching Black males how to adjust to stigma, racism, and discrimination by making an intentional effort to aim their struggles at the areas of their personality that have the most cognitive muscle. This channeling of struggle assists the Black male in effectively sustaining productive functioning and adjusting "life-flexing".

When a Black male has a predetermined outline for managing and utilizing his strengths, he is preparing himself with a system of ideas, concepts, and framing processes that will allow him to accomplish the series of psychological steps necessary to thrive despite extreme social resistance. This utilization of acquired mental, emotional, and spiritual muscle serves as an internal fortitude and foundation for responding to life in a racist environment. These newly acquired cognitive muscles again can be transported and utilized as a means of remaining resilient in the face of future life challenges. By keeping the Black male thinking, feeling, and participating in the process of utilizing his growth in the areas of emotional intelligence, problem solving, and conflict resolution, you are realigning his trajectory towards self-awareness, self-actualization, and a positive self-image.

Stabilize

Most of a Black male's dysfunctional behaviors come from insecurities that are birthed out of unmet socio-emotional needs. These insecurities are the fuel that drive Black dysfunctionality and destructive decision-making patterns. Systems by nature resist change. Utilizing the internal strengths and external resources available to Black male clients is pivotal in order to sustain optimal functioning. This system modification is accomplished via the correcting of misperceptions that hinder attempts towards forming a positive identity, making good decisions, and living a life of meaning and purpose. When working to psychologically Stabilize the Black male, you are essentially working to build into his mind the capacity to sustain productive functioning in a racially-dysfunctional environment.

In order for a Black male to sustain equilibrium or productive functioning in such a socially assaultive environment, he must be taught how to utilize intentional fortitude and guided resilience. Furthermore, he will need to become capable of psychologically preparing for racially-charged social experiences by having a pre-determined plan for remaining mentally and emotionally stable when tasked with the process of interpreting and filtering experiences of racism, stigma, and discrimination. The goal is to foster within the client the ability to psychologize his racial encounters through the lens of confidence and hope. Finally, in order for the Black male client to remain psychologically stabilized, he will need to effectively utilize his external resources and assertively access his support network.

Desensitize

The tumultuous emotional experiences produced by the acceptance of responsibility in the face of social discrimination can sometimes serve as a failure trigger for those who are trying to pursue success while at the same time deal with the fear of having what they will work so hard to attain withheld or taken away. It is important that a Black male develops the cognitive tolerance necessary to cope with the fears and emotions that accompany pursuing progress – *otherwise he will malfunction and the Dream will diminish.*

The goal of the Desensitization phase in the SIT driven ALP approach is to assist the Black male in constructing a strategy for desensitizing himself from negative environmental elements. In the Desensitization phase, a plan is established for self-management in order to protect the client from internalizing and identifying with the many negative elements seeking to negatively define his personhood and his future. Furthermore, this decreased psychological sensitivity to general life-stress, as well as race-related stress, will work to decrease the Black male client's chances of retreating into maladaptive coping and other forms of destructive emotion management.

In this phase it is pivotal for the client to understand that he has a history of functioning and responding to reality in a counter-productive manner as a result of social conditioning. As the client begins to conceptualize his dysfunction and underachievement through the lens of stigmatic conditioning, he is becoming more competent at connecting moments of poor decision-making to social engineering and cultural conditioning.

The awareness of the ability of past memories of stigma to stunt positive development can help motivate the Black male client to take responsibility for modifying how he responds to life and reality. In this stage, the client has to create an area of psychological defense that prepares him to protect himself from being overwhelmed by the sadness, anger, and anxiety he may experience as a result of feeling powerless, socially abused, and abandoned. If this psychological defense system is not in place and the client is not desensitized to stigmatic elements, he will resort to the compulsive use of dysfunctional coping when encountering uncomfortable emotions.

Desensitization requires a therapist to help the Black male client develop a thorough understanding of both his internal triggers (perceptual and emotional) and his external triggers (people, places, things, and events). This understanding will endow the client with the ego strength and voluntary control neccessary to take control of his response style and decision-making when facing life hardships. Without this ego strength and voluntary control, a client will, out of a compulsive need for emotional pain-alleviation, use people, places, things, and behaviors as a means of self-medicating. If left unchecked, this can lead to an addiction to relationships, dysfunctional behaviors, and dysfunctional habits.

In Black males, people, places, and things are both consciously and subconsciously used to manage the pain that comes with national rejection, loneliness, and isolation. Debilitating levels of stress, anxiety, and fear can be produced when a Black male begins to invest personal energy in long-term goals that can be potentially denied. In an effort to alleviate this stress and anxiety he may begin to consciously and subconsciously self-sabotage his progress. This lapse into failure and ultimate relief from stress can become an addictive cycle of failure. Therefore, Desensitization requires decreasing the client's psychological vulnerability. Desensitization also requires the deliberate construction of a failure relapse prevention strategy. Thic failure relapse prevention stategy is critical for the accomplishing of psychological invulnerability.

Psychological Processing = Re-thinking, Re-feeling, Re-responding

When utilizing the SIT driven ALP approach for empowering Black males, a therapist must have the primary goal of empowering the client to take control of his response system when navigating his stigmatic maze. The client takes control of his response style by not allowing the environment to incite counterproductive decision-making. In order for a therapist to recondition a Black male's response system to stigma, he or she must confront any internal doubts regarding the Black male client's ability to learn the skills necessary to master his stigmatizing environment and thrive in his harsh reality.

The SIT guided ALP intervention is all about re-psychologizing stigmatic messages and events that stir up negative emotions and incite counterproductive behavior. The SIT guided ALP process strategically works to help the Black male client reframe his life experiences by giving his experiences positive meaning, which will by default, inspire him to sustain productive functioning.

These newfound empowering meanings and interpretations act as narratives that define and explain reality to the embattled Black male. These newfound personal definitions of reality operate as mental frameworks of hope, purpose, and inspiration. These messages also operate as filters by blocking out disempowering interpretational residue and only allowing empowering interpretations to flow through to the Black male client's Self-System, Value-System, and Belief-System. When counseling Black males, the essential goal of therapy is to empower the client to be able to respond to stigmatizing and discriminatory events, encounters, and experiences in a productive and non-self-sabotaging manner. This goal becomes a possibility once the therapist is successful at helping the client associate racially-charged experiences with opportunities to prove to himself and the rest of the world that he is able to overcome race-related obstacles on his path.

The gears of our psychological system (how we psychologize) are the driving forces of our life-progress, life-fulfillment, and life-happiness. How we psychologize represents how we perceive, interpret, organize, relate to, and give explanation to our life and reality. Our system of thinking, feeling, and behaving is both challenged and reinforced by information gathered from experiences and events. Counseling is an instrument that can aid Black males in the process of uploading positive information, which challenges the negative information that may be sustaining a system of dysfunctionality. These pieces of positive information and meaning are connected like a puzzle to create new perceptions, beliefs, and meanings.

This re-psychologizing process leads to modified interpretations, assimilations, and associations that can now be contextualized around these new meanings. Once reformulated, these new meanings are integrated into the Self-System, Belief-System, and Value-System and ultimately empower the thinking, feeling, and behaving networks of the psychological system. This system of thinking, feeling, and behaving will ultimately empower the Black male client to overcome his complicated experiences with racism, stigma, and discrimination.

The SIT driven ALP approach is not about teaching a Black male client to blame all of his problems on racism. The SIT driven ALP approach is about helping a Black male become aware of the fact that some of his disempowering perceptions, uncomfortable emotions, and dysfunctional behaviors may be related to his life-long exposures to racism, stigma, and discrimination.

In some cases the topic of racism, stigma, and discrimination will never arise in a therapy session. It is most important however that a therapist recognizes that a good portion of a Black male's presenting issues will be directly and/or indirectly related to his exposure to the stigmatizing elements of racism. Many Black males will refuse to acknowledge the impact or racism, stigma, and discrimination on their happiness and life progress. They have been indoctrinated to believe that if they do acknowledge the impact of racism they are making excuses for themselves.

Even an entry level therapist understands that it is virtually impossible for any mind to travel through such a maze of rejection and alienation and not come out on the other side scarred and affected. So again, acknowledging the impact of racism is not making an excuse for all of a Black male's problems. Furthermore, the acknowledgement of racism does not have to be the primary topic of any given therapy session with a Black male client. What is of utmost importance when conceptualizing a Black male's presenting problem is that the therapist understands that in most cases, a good portion of his underachievement issues will be related to internalized racism.

Creating Racially-Appropriate Therapeutic Environments

The SIT driven ALP model functions on the principal that Black males have race-specific social experiences, which lead to race-specific psychological experiences, which in turn has historically led to race-specific social underachievement issues in Black males. The SIT driven ALP model is designed to reverse or at best minimize the impact of stigmatizing developmental experiences by providing Black males with a platform for experiencing psychological empowerment via racially-appropriate psychotherapy.

The SIT driven ALP model is a racially-contextualized model strategically designed to meet the race-specific psychosocial needs of Black males. This holistic approach for addressing the psychological needs of Black males functions as a programmatic therapeutic curriculum that utilizes qualitative risk analysis, resource matching, case management, relational learning, and prescriptive activities as a means of curtailing underperformance. The SIT guided ALP model strategically engages the evolving Black male client with a deeply probing questioning sequence. The SIT guided ALP approach also utilizes enriching developmental activities and exercises that programmatically build into the Black male mind the psychological skill set and developmental assets necessary for positive life outcomes. This leading practice can be integrated into any counselor's already established process for fostering Black male success. The SIT driven ALP intervention can also function as a standalone procedure for counseling Black males. The racially-contextualized questioning sequence and developmental exercises that make up the SIT Driven ALP approach represent a type of therapeutic psychoeducational curriculum as it merges racially-contextualized therapy with racially-contextualized activities and exercises.

Rationale for the SIT-ALP Therapeutic Model

The unresponsiveness of Black males to traditional methods of psychotherapy is a clear indication that traditional psychological approaches lack the capacity to pick up enough pieces of the fragmented Black male to improve his chances of adequate social performance. The field of psychology must make a deliberate effort to provide contextualized therapeutic modalities (racially-appropriate guided questioning, information, ideas, people, support, resources, social networks, etc.) that are capable of building the psychological skill set (hope, motivation, focus, resilience, impulse control, ability to delay gratification, confidence, etc.) required for sustained engagement with the process of achieving success. Until this moral mandate is truly pursued, the field of psychology will never have the capacity necessary to effectively treat Black males. Therapy has the awesome potential of playing a significant role in psyche-shaping and human development. With this in mind, therapists should make it a professional and moral obligation to provide Black males with a therapeutic environment capable of fostering positive development and reversing the Black male's trajectory toward social failure.

Race-Specific Social Experiences Produce Race-Specific Psychological Experiences which Produce Race-Specific Therapeutic Needs

Race-specific social experiences produce race-specific psychological experiences which produce race-specific therapeutic needs. A Black male's race-specific psychosocial needs cannot be addressed by using out of the box, cookie-cutter therapeutic modalities. These race-specific psychosocial needs can only be addressed through the strategic researching and developing of race-specific therapeutic models for treating Black males. This is how science works and science trumps tradition.

When counseling systems ignore science and neglect to provide race-specific methods for treating Black males, they are unethically immersing clients in psychosocially restricted environments, which ultimately result in restricted opportunities for change. To prevent such an inequitable situation, the SIT guided ALP model strategically works to meet the race-specific therapeutic needs of Black males.

The SIT guided ALP model is a prescriptive intervention designed to reverse the negative mental and emotional effects of being barraged by racialized experiences, stigmatic messaging, and discriminatory practices. The SIT guided ALP model does not ignore the statistically proven fact that Black males comprise the most stigmatized category of America citizen. Due to this social reality, Black males need specific psychological strengths and skill sets that other categories of American citizens do not need in order to achieve positive life outcomes. With this guiding principle in mind, the primary desired outcome of the SIT guided ALP model is the development of a new Belief-System, Value-System, and Self-System via psychological re-conditioning.

The goal of psychological re-conditioning is strategically approached using racially-appropriate treatment modalities for engaging Black males in relational learning via racially-contextualized therapy. Most counseling systems lack the cultural capacity necessary to treat Black males. A culturally incompetent counseling environment is a counseling environment that does not implement a racially-specific strategy for treating Black males. Such counseling systems habitually construct therapeutic environments that utilize techniques that ignore the fact that people discover, understand, and express themselves through the lens of their race and culture. In contrast a racially-appropriate counseling environment considers the social and psychological experiences of the consumer of the intervention. A racially-competent therapeutic approach strategically researches and develops interventions to treat the symptoms of Black male underachievement that are deeply rooted in their unceasing stigmatizing psychosocial experiences.

Race-Appropriate Structure and Functioning

As mentioned in Part 1 of this book, racism, stigma, and discrimination have resulted in deep histories of failure, disappointment, vulnerability, poverty, set-backs, and unmet socio-emotional needs for Black males. These harsh developmental experiences necessitate a strategic immersion in a therapeutic environment that possesses racially-appropriate stimuli (i.e. people, questioning, information, ideas, activities, experiences, historical context, motivational cues, etc.) that address the client's race-specific needs.

As previously discussed, Black boys slowly and sequentially prepare themselves for failure and have subconsciously given themselves permission to live out the social prophecy of underachievement. If these young minds are not strategically and immediately engaged in positive developmental experiences during late adolescence or young adulthood, they will consciously as well as subconsciously look for signs of failure and opportunities to escape responsibility. So, what does the SIT therapeutic model do to shield these young beautiful minds from a social prophecy that has served as a cultural curse haunting them for essentially all their lives?

The SIT therapeutic model is guided by the principle that the Belief-System, Value-System, and Self-System work together to determine perceptions and those perceptions ultimately determine a client's response system. With this in mind, it can be theorized that as a result of destructive internalization, Black boys psychologically evolve into Black men who perceive themselves, the world, life, and the future through a perceptual lens of negativity, pessimism, doubt, and alienation. Ultimately, in the face of situations or challenges that require hope, the hopeless Black male is statistically more likely to respond with maladaptive coping strategies such as escapism, avoidance, and self-sabotage.

In the spirit of this theory and reasoning, the immediate goal of the SIT therapeutic model is to re-condition, re-engineer, re-build, and re-program the Belief -System, Value-System, and Self-

System of the Black male. The chart below represents a statistically appropriate risk analysis for a 16-year-old African American male client.

A Case Study and Risk Analysis:
Marcus is a 16-year-old Black Male

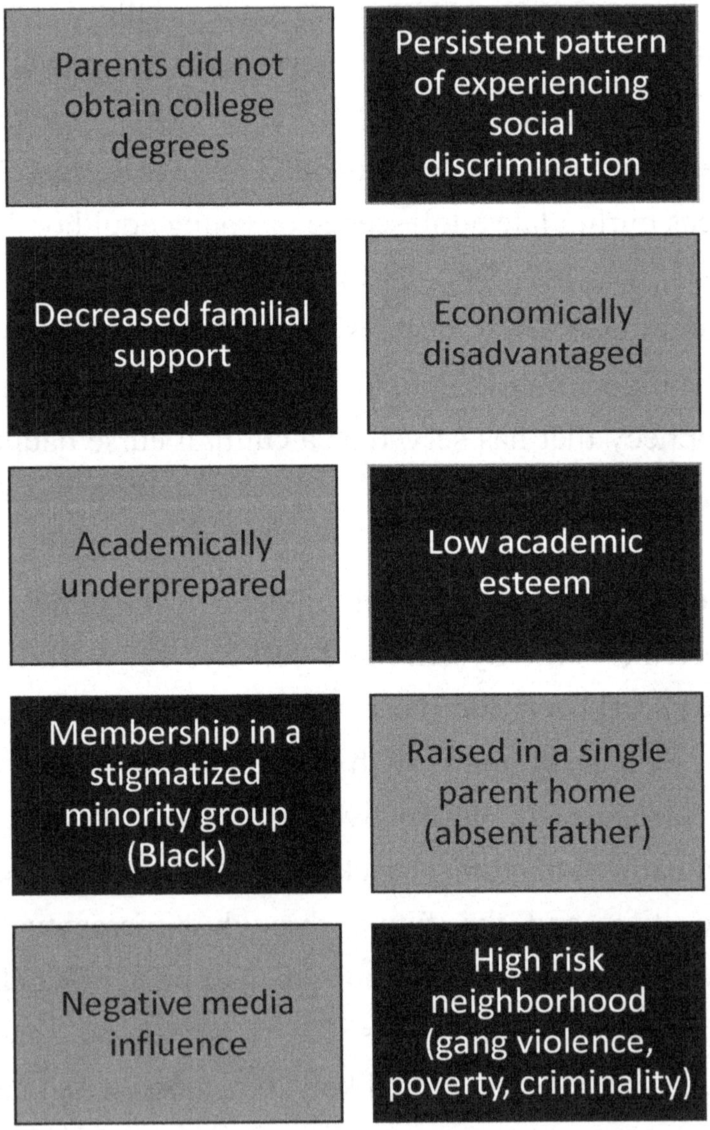

Note: Although Marcus has an array of statistically appropriate risks, his biggest risk as it relates to psychological empowerment, as with most Black males, is Internalized Stigma.

Empowering and Reconditioning the Black Male Soul: An SIT Guided Approach to Helping Marcus

As a result of Marcus' developmental experiences, he will more than likely encounter underachievement issues that are directly and/or indirectly connected to issues of stigma, poverty, academic under-preparedness, low academic esteem, an absentee father, and attachment to a negative social network. These issues will produce a sense of hopelessness, anxiety, low expectations, a negative worldview, and a negative self-view. This will in turn trigger a failure reflex that will produce escaping behaviors such as withdrawal or self-sabotage. The purpose of the SIT therapeutic model is to re-habilitate, re-condition, and re-shape Marcus' Belief-System, Value-System, and Self-System, which will in turn improve his chances of achieving both academic and social success.

The Driving Philosophy of the SIT Model

The SIT therapeutic model describes the therapeutic relationship as a persuasive re-conditioning relationship between a Black male (Marcus) and a professional therapist. The primary purpose of this re-conditioning relationship is fostering the transmission of information and inspiration via relational learning. This platform of relational learning has the specific purpose of reconditioning the Belief System, Value System, and Self-System of the Black male (Marcus).

Despite the presence of seemingly infinite amount of models and approaches for fostering change, the SIT therapeutic model assumes that racially-contextualized relational learning via counseling is necessary for fostering measurable positive outcomes in Black males. This racially-contextualized relational learning via counseling is the master gear that powers the majority of the change accomplished by the SIT process. In short, consistent, genuine interactions with a professional therapist and consistent engagement in activities and exercises that facilitate mental and emotional empowerment, appears to be the most active ingredient or potent component of the SIT therapeutic model for counseling Black males.

Preferred Characteristics of the SIT Therapist

Over the course of my counseling career I have been blessed to gather and sort through an extensive amount of qualitative data as a result of engaging in hundreds of hours of structured dialogue, intensive counseling, and strategic success coaching with hundreds of Black males (adolescents and adults). These in-depth counseling interactions have helped me discover that the majority of change generated through the therapeutic process when working with Black males, is mediated by five key counselor traits and counseling conditions. The upcoming pages will outline the counselor traits and counseling conditions necessary for the creation of a re-conditioning relationship.

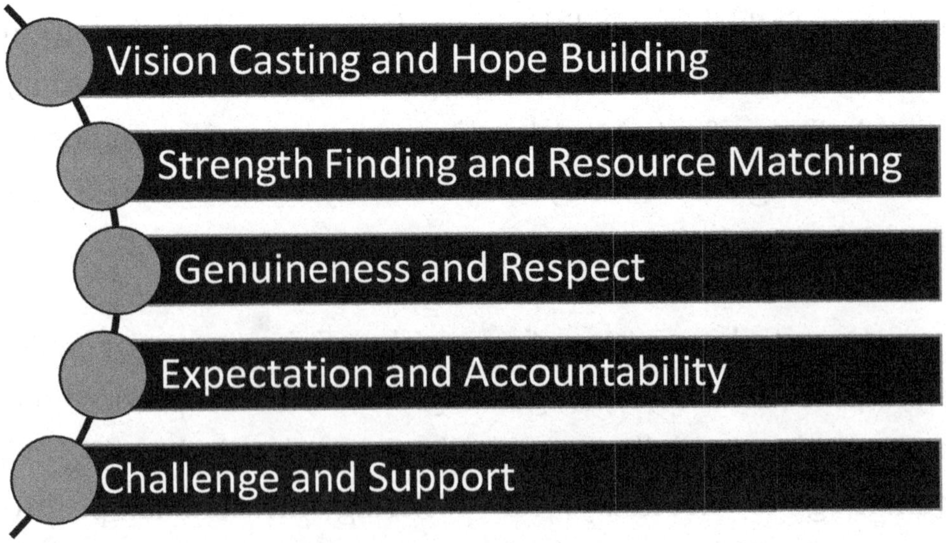

Vision Casting and Hope Building

A vision is a "desired future reality". A personal dream or vision should be the most inspirational element in anyone's life. An immediate responsibility of a therapist includes providing Marcus with an opportunity to map out exactly what he wants his future to look like as it relates to lifestyle, career, finances, educational goals, etc. An effective counselor sees vision casting as a platform for helping Marcus clearly define his personal dream and vision for life. Once his vision is psychologically conceived, it serves as a type of map, destination, and voice that constantly reminds Marcus of the importance of hard work, perseverance, good decision-making, and most of all not internalizing stigmatic messaging.

Due to a profoundly insidious history of stigma and disappointment, many Black males have been stripped of their efficacy and confidence. This lack of confidence negatively impacts the ability of Black males to dream of a prosperous and satisfying future. In therapy it is pivotal that Marcus' hope be constantly restored and his personal vision frequently reinforced. By providing Marcus with the opportunity to map out or script his future, a therapist is moving him out of the daydreaming phase and into the action phase of the vision building process.

The SIT therapeutic model sees the therapeutic relationship as a great platform for vision and hope building. In this relationship a therapist serves as a type of co-pilot who helps Marcus navigate his way towards his vision, which will hopefully minimize Marcus' chances of "losing his way". As an assistant vision-caster, the counselor is effectively re-wiring Marcus to not only desire success, but to also believe that success is possible. Such hope and belief will minimize Marcus' chances of giving up on his American Dream.

Strength Finding and Resource Matching

When counseling Marcus, an effective therapist places a priority on focusing on the strengths and resources Marcus already has at his disposal in contrast to focusing on Marcus' psychological shortcomings. This type of therapeutic approach will naturally activate the internal resources Marcus will need to overcome his life challenges.

By helping Marcus identify and utilize the psychological resources in which he is endowed, Marcus is being made more capable of accessing the inner resources he will eventually need to accomplish his life goals. These psychological resources include persistence, openness, faith, optimism, hope, readiness for change, and personal responsibility. External social supports include the people, places, and things that can positively influence Marcus's life trajectory (e.g. membership in an informational, inspirational, and supportive organization).

Genuineness and Respect

An effective therapist has to integrate relationship-building dialogue carefully and deliberately into the therapeutic sessions. The information and inspiration transmitted via the therapeutic relationship serves as a master switch for engaging the gears of success inside of Marcus. The inherent strengths and abilities that are triggered as a result of being engaged in a genuine, respectful, accepting, and empathetic relationship serves as a type of operational bridge of relational communication that mediates the connection between the counseling process and Marcus' re-conditioning.

Expectation and Accountability

The purpose of expectation is to guide decision-making. Expectations often determine a person's level of personal effort and investment. In the very early stages of the therapeutic relationship, Marcus and his counselor will work together to mutually establish clearly defined counseling goals and life expectations. This definitive outline of expectations works to provide Marcus with concrete measures of accomplishment and accountability. As it relates to expectations and accountability, a therapist serves as a mirror of duty and responsibility, reflecting back to the Marcus his personal obligation to be accountable for his actions and give an answer for any behavior incongruent with his established expectations. Exposure to highly interactive therapeutic exchanges that consistently reinforce expectations, will serve as a strong voice of accountability, which can empower Marcus to consistently produce the level of energy, focus, and dedication necessary to achieve his life goals.

Challenge and Support

For Marcus, the primary purpose of the therapeutic relationship is to promote positive personal, social, and educational growth. Positive growth cannot be achieved without a balanced psychological interplay of challenge and support between the therapist and the client. A therapist's primary job is to serve as a major source of psychosocial capital. As a respected and validated source of information and inspiration, Marcus' therapist has to appropriately challenge his dysfunctional expressions, misguided values, excuse making, and general weaknesses all while supporting and comforting the growing pains associated with re-conditioning, hard work, and forward progress.

The Power of Racially-Contextualized Therapy!

For Marcus, it's about being in a therapeutic environment where patterns of purposeful communication can routinely take place. It is about providing Marcus with an opportunity to evolve in a setting that allows for the exchange of optimistic perspectives and empowering viewpoints. This is of utmost importance as Black males, all too often, come from a network of information and ideas that are devoid of empowerment, optimism, and purpose. With this in mind, the therapeutic setting serves as an affirming and challenging space for Marcus to not only be held accountable for his personal success, but this setting can also serve as a space for Marcus to be exposed to positive messages about himself, his life, and his future. In this stigma-conscious therapeutic relationship, Marcus is constantly reinforced to take responsibility, work hard, and seek help when necessary. Furthermore, Marcus and his therapist must have a shared understanding of what is acceptable and expected of their therapeutic relationship.

A Case for Racially-Appropriate Interventions

A therapist who is racially-neglectful assumes there is no need to deliver racially-appropriate strategies. This type of therapist believes singular techniques and interventions can be universally applied to all subgroups of American citizens. Racially-insensitive therapists ignore the fact that people discover and understand themselves and their lives through the lens of their physical characteristics and social experiences. A racially-appropriate intervention is an intervention that strategically considers the demographically specific psychosocial experiences of the Black male client. This racially-sensitive understanding is critical when developing a strategy for addressing Marcus' psychological needs. It makes scientific sense to assume that if psychosocial forces play a part in the development of stigmatic symptoms, then psychosocial forces also have the capacity to play a part in the alleviation of stigmatic symptoms. If environmental forces are responsible for counterproductive conditioning, then environmental forces can also produce productive conditioning.

Those who are racially-insensitive assume that everyone should be able to have access to the exact same resources and achieve the exact same progress, results, and outcomes. This assumption comes from the seat of Majority privilege. Those with Majority privilege lack an awareness of the race-specific social experiences of American Minorities. Racially-insensitive individuals admit that, yes Black males have less opportunities and resources, but yet in the same breath these individuals will say Black males should not receive even the smallest amount of specialized resource allocation to catch up to other citizens, who by social default, had more opportunities since birth. Let me be clear, it is not necessarily my position that extra monies and allocations be spent on supplementing the Black male struggle. It is however, my strong position that a fair and equal amount of resources be spent on specialized educational and therapeutic models that have been proven through practice and/or research to effectively empower, educate, and foster change in Black males.

The Art and Science of Repairing, Restoring, and Reconditioning a Boy Named Marcus

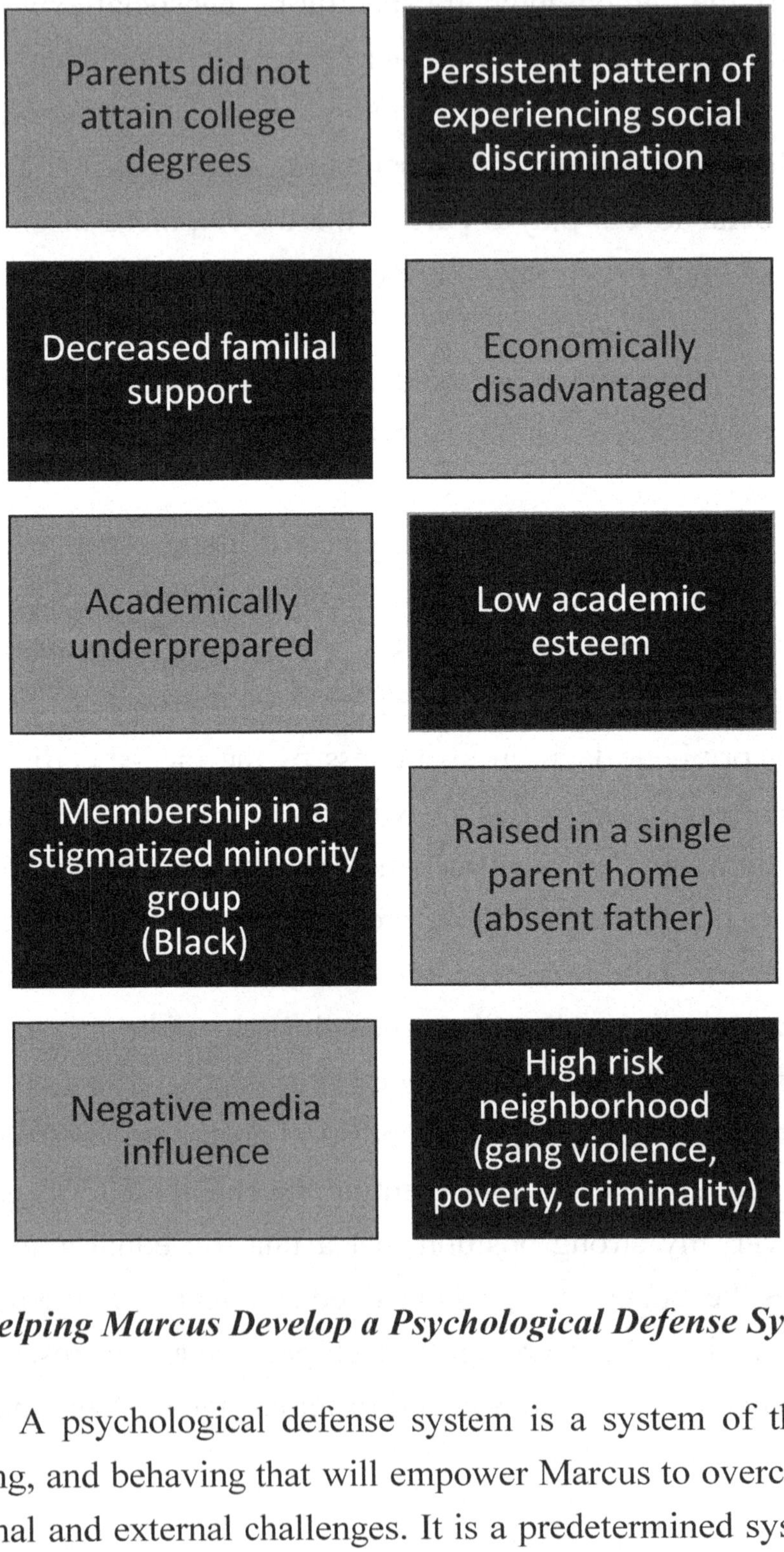

Helping Marcus Develop a Psychological Defense System

A psychological defense system is a system of thinking, feeling, and behaving that will empower Marcus to overcome his internal and external challenges. It is a predetermined system for productively coping with the internal and external triggers that can compel him to engage in dysfunctional stigmatic behavior. This productive coping includes the use of counseling, support system utilization, access to psychoeducation, and the identification and application of Marcus' psychological strengths. A list of trigger alleviation strategies is below:

Trigger Alleviation Strategies

Vision Casting

Vision Casting is the deliberate outlining of what Marcus desires for his future reality. Vision Casting essentially outlines Marcus' long-term goals in eight specific areas of his human experience (spirituality, relationships, emotional well-being, health and wellness, finances, education, career, and humanitarianism).

Meaning Making

Meaning Making is an intentional effort to review and analyze life challenges with the ultimate goals of finding meaning, purpose, and the learning of life lessons. It is an opportunity for Marcus to engage in the process of identifying the positive outcomes that have resulted from his negative and hurtful experiences.

Social Network Purging

Social Network Purging is the deliberate reviewing and analyzing of the people and/or groups of people that negatively impact how Marcus thinks, feels, and behaves. Purging the social network is done in an attempt to remove relational influences that negatively influence Marcus' Belief-System, Value-System, and Self-System.

Trigger Avoidance Plan

A trigger avoidance plan outlines a specific strategy that Marcus will use to avoid the people, places, things, and scenarios that typically trigger the use of destructive perceptions, negative emotions, and dysfunctional behavior. The use of a trigger avoidance plan will minimize the chances of Marcus placing himself in positions where his psychological vulnerabilities are exposed and his weaknesses are more likely to take control of his decision-making.

Reality Response Script

A reality response script is a pre-determined method for mentally, emotionally, and behaviorally responding to people, places, things, and events that normally cause Marcus to engage in bad decision-making. A reality response script can be an internal method of thinking (framing and/or interpreting) or an external manner of behaviorally responding to triggering situations, thoughts, and emotions. A reality response script is a pre-determined strategy of expressing or managing uncomfortable emotions. For example, Marcus will prepare and practice a verbal response in situations where his peers tell him that he is "acting White" or not being a "real nigga". Example: When my friends say that I am lame or acting White when I focus on my school work I will say "a dumb person is a broke person" or I will say "when did being dumb become cool" or I will say "how has not taking care of your schoolwork helped you and your future".

Optimistic Visualization

Optimistic visualization can take place in the present-tense as well as the future-tense and is the process of mentally imagining positive outcomes to various life scenarios. The purpose of optimistic visualization is to help recondition Marcus' Belief-System, Self-System, and Value-System by replacing negative thoughts with building blocks of positive images, which will increase Marcus' level of optimism, hope, and emotional empowerment.

Positive Life-Statement List

A positive Life-Statement List involves the strategic and routine use of verbal affirmations to positively define the person they are and the person they will become. It serves the purpose of replacing the negative thoughts that Marcus may have about himself and his future.

Self-Discovery Journal

A Self-Discovery Journal provides Marcus with an opportunity to routinely summarize and analyze the people, places, things, and events that both positively and negatively impact his thoughts, feelings, and behaviors. Such a self-discovery journal will empower Marcus by giving him a sense of control over both his internal and external realities.

Relaxation Techniques

Relaxation Techniques provide Marcus with a pre-determined list of activities that may alleviate the anxiety and stress that may come as a result of negative thoughts, emotions, and life experiences. In the face of stress, anxiety, and sadness, relaxation techniques provide Marcus an opportunity to calm down, properly assess his situation, and respond in a manner that is both positive and productive.

Resource and Support System Utilization Strategy

A Resource and Support System Utilization Strategy outlines the exact days, times, and frequency for which Marcus will utilize specific resources available to aid his personal improvement, empowerment, and forward progress.

Expressive Arts

Expressice Arts represent activities that are designed to provide Marcus with a healthy outlet for expressing powerfully uncomfortable emotions. Such helpful forms of expression help to minimize the potential for Marcus to allow his emotions to create problems in his life. It also gives Marcus a specific target for channeling his powerful emotions into productive works of art. These works of art can eventually not only empower Marcus but also empower other people who will be exposed to his artistic creations.

Hobby Appointments

Hobby Appointments serve the purpose of providing Marcus with an escape route or a means of avoiding negative thoughts and emotions. It is a healthy distraction from some of the pain that may accompany difficult situations that Marcus either has no control over or presently lacks the skill or willpower to overcome.

Music Therapy

Music Therapy psychologically engages Marcus with words, melodies, meaningful lyrics, and rhythmic vibrations that can effectively alter his negative emotional states and trigger a sense of energy, empowerment, and hope. Marcus' therapist should encourage him to create musical playlists that are empowering and mood altering.

Inspirational Movie Viewing

Inspirational Movie Viewing provides Marcus with an opportunity to observe the formula or approach that other resilient individuals have used to overcome significant life challenges. It is an opportunity for a type of virtual resilience role-modeling that Marcus can observe and emulate. Such inspirational stories of heroism and victory on the part of others can encourage Marcus to take control of his reality. Inspirational movies also can give Marcus a sense of power over his decision-making as well as his eventual life outcome. Finally, inspirational movies can be very effective at helping Marcus find meaning and purpose in his life struggles. When Marcus observes another individual experiencing hardship, embracing their struggle, and ultimately bringing glory to their struggle, it serves as a psychological blueprint which Marcus can follow on his road to overcoming life obstacles.

At various points of therapy, the therapist should work with Marcus to identify Trigger Alleviation Activities that can empower him to avoid internalizing racism and consistently engage in productive decision-making. These activities do not have to be solely designed around Marcus' experiences with racism. They can also be designed to enhance other general areas of Marcus' life (i.e. self-esteem, relationships, motivation, etc.). In whatever ways these activities are utilized, the therapist at various points and stages should review the effectiveness of the Trigger Alleviation Activities utilized by the client.

Stigma Internalization Therapy (SIT)
Guided Movement from Stigmatic Determinism to Responsibility and Resilience
(Fifteen 60-Minute Counseling Sessions)

SESSION 1

PROBLEM EXPLORATION Part 1

Verbalize

THERAPIST: "So let's talk about your life as it is right now. What parts of your life would you like to discuss, spread on the table, sort out, and put back together in a way in which the problem is either eliminated or you learn how to cope with your situation? There are two types of people in this world. People who allow their struggles to make them better and people who allow their struggles to make them worse. You and I will be spending the next few months working to create a strategy to make sure this situation makes you a stronger, wiser and better person. Now, having said all that, why are you here today?"

1. In your own words what are the two biggest challenges in your life?
2. What makes these two problems so challenging?
3. How have they negatively affected your progression in school, life, and your personal relationships?
4. How long have these problems existed?
5. When did you realize that these were problems?

Intellectualize

THERAPIST: "So let's think deeply about the things that are going on in your life. All problems have a source or something that keeps the problem alive. The environment use people, places, and things to feed our problems and keep them alive. As it relates to yourself, you keep your problems alive with how you think, feel, and respond to life. We are going to use our brains to help you develop a strategy that will help you overcome the things within you and within your environment that both cause and feed the problems you are currently facing."

1. Why do you think these problems exist?
2. What proof do you have that this is the cause of your problems?
3. How often do you think about these problems?
4. How do you feel when you think about these problems?
5. When do these problems typically occur (i.e. what triggers the client's current problems?)
6. When do these current problems seem to be at their worst?
7. What do you do to deal with the stress, strain, and frustration of these problems?
8. Why do you think you respond in this manner?
9. How are your thoughts about yourself affected by these problems?
10. How are your thoughts about your life and your future affected by these problems?
11. How does this way of responding effect your life and your relationships?
12. What are your goals as it relates to solving these problems?

Emotionalize

THERAPIST: "I am sure you are experiencing a lot of different emotions because of your current life struggles. We all know that guys are trained to not express emotions and feelings about the things that are troubling them. As human beings, however, it is important that you can acknowledge not only how you see, interpret, and understand your life issues but it is also important to come to grips with how these issues have emotionally impacted you as it relates to the fears, frustrations, sadness, and anger you are experiencing as a result of your situation. Let's spend the next few minutes discussing how you feel about the struggles you are currently facing."

1. What part of your problems seem to be totally out of your control?
2. What part of your problems do you feel you are responsible for creating?
3. What part of your problems are most frustrating?
4. What is the most hurtful part of this situation?
5. Do you ever feel angry about this situation?
6. How do you deal with this anger?
7. Do you ever feel sad about this situation?
8. How do you deal with this sadness?
9. Have the emotions surrounding these problems ever caused you to make a bad decision?
10. Give me two examples of when your emotions caused you to make a bad decision.
11. How did you feel after you made this decision?
12. How are you feeling right now as we talk about your situation?
13. Usually, when you think or talk about your situation, how long do you feel this way?
14. How would you prefer to feel when you think about or talk about this situation in the future?
15. What do you think it will take to avoid feeling upset in the future when you think about or talk about this situation?

Spiritualize

THERAPIST: "Using the philosophy or logic that assumes everything happens for a reason and everything has some type of purpose, let's work to discover the meaning or the reason why you are in this life situation. It is crucial that you find purpose and meaning in your struggle. It is important that you embrace the fact that this struggle can help to make you a better person. If you do not find meaning in your struggle, you are going to feel like a victim and believe that life has no rhyme or reason and only serves the purpose of making you miserable. If you think in this manner about your situation, your struggle will not make you stronger but instead, this situation will make you weaker. So for the next few minutes we are going to work together to find meaning, purpose, and positivity in your struggles."

1. In the big picture of life, why do you think this is happening to you?
2. What are two great things that can happen because of this situation?
3. How can you use this struggle to help others?
4. How has this problem affected your perception of your Higher Power?
5. How do you feel this problem is connected to your purpose in life?
6. What part of this problem should you turn over to your Higher Power?
7. How has your Higher Power helped you with this situation?

Post Session Activity

Optimistic Visualization: "For the next seven days, I want you to spend three minutes per day visualizing a successful life. I want you to imagine your life getting better and how you will feel when your problems are resolved and you have accomplished your personal goals. You can do this exercise in your room with the lights off and motivational music playing in the background or anywhere else you feel comfortable and are free from distraction."

> Note: The client should be advised to set a visualization reminder alert on his cell phone.

Therapist Provides Session Summary

At the conclusion of each session, a therapist using the ALP driven SIT model should provide a client with a clear outline of what has taken place in the therapy session. The session summary should be a brief review of the most critical points, experiences, and pieces of information that may have emerged during the session. The session summary should be concise, yet clear, concrete, and definitive. A typical session summary will include a review of the client's presenting problem, the impact of the problem on the client's life, goals for the session, an identified hypothesis for the cause of the problem, identified strengths and strategies for overcoming the presenting problem, and a review of any assigned post-session activities. The therapist should be careful to provide the client with a handwritten summary of the session. By providing the client with a handwritten outline of what has transpired in any given therapy session, a therapist is increasing the client's ability to recall critical psychosocial information, gain post-session insight, and follow through on any established strategies for overcoming their presenting problem.

SESSION 2

PROBLEM EXPLORATION Part 2 & VISION CASTING

Prior Session Visualization Activity Checkpoint

Actualize

THERAPIST: "Have you ever heard the saying 'that which does not kill you only makes you stronger?' It is very important that you do not let this situation make you weak and vulnerable. As I told you before, there are two types of people in this world. There are some people who when something bad happens they become worse than they were before the situation occurred. There are other people who, when something bad happens, they actually become a better person. It is important that you allow this struggle to make you stronger for future responsibilities and higher levels of living."

"It is important that you see this trouble as building something inside of you that is going to help you in the future. What I am saying is that there are things in the future that you are destined to accomplish. These future accomplishments require certain strengths and abilities that you will only gain from struggle. These strengths and abilities that you are gaining now will cause you to be able to handle the stress and pressure that will come as a result of having to accomplish even greater things in the future. In other words, if you did not have these current struggles you would not have what it takes in the future to be successful. Now if you just let life happen to you, you will not become a better person. In contrast, if you embrace your struggle and perceive it as an opportunity to develop within yourself the psychological muscles that will make you more effective in your future life responsibilities, you will have successfully worked to make this issue something that has made you a better person."

1. What knowledge and wisdom about yourself have you gained as a result of the issues we have discussed?
2. What knowledge and wisdom about life have you gained as a result of the issues we have been discussing?
3. What have you grown to like more about yourself because of these issues?
4. What strengths have you acquired as a result of the issues we have discussed today?
5. How has this situation made you a better person?
6. Does having these strengths and abilities make you feel better about yourself as a person?
7. Does having these strengths and abilities make you feel better about your future?

Utilize

THERAPIST: "Now that we have identified the strengths, talents, abilities, and skills your life struggles have brought you, let's talk about ways in which we can use these strengths to deal with or overcome your current problems. Also, let's discuss how your strengths can be used as a means of overcoming some of your other life issues we have not discussed."

1. Thinking about the strengths and knowledge you have acquired over the course of life, how can you use these strengths to overcome the challenges we have discussed today?
2. What barriers do you think you will encounter as you work to solve these problems?
3. What strengths, skills, and knowledge will you use to

overcome these barriers?

4. As it relates to some of the bad decisions you have made, how can your strengths help you to overcome the moments in which you usually make bad decisions?
5. How do you think these newfound strengths, abilities, and areas of knowledge can help you in your pursuit of success?
6. How can you use the knowledge and strengths you have gained to help other people?
7. Can you think of anyone in your life circle who you can use your strengths to help overcome their current life problems?

Stabilize

THERAPIST: "Okay, so we have talked about and thought about a lot of things. We have also talked about your feelings and brought purpose to your struggle. Finally, we have not only identified some of the strengths you have acquired as a result of your life, but we have also talked about how you can use these strengths to overcome your current and future life challenges."

"Now let's talk about how you are going to not only think and feel better but also how you are going to achieve and maintain balance and the ability to adjust to life and reality. Essentially, we will work to develop a strategy for achieving a level of mental and emotional adaption that allows you to sustain productive functioning even when you are facing tough situations. Let's take a few minutes to discuss a few strategies to improve your ability to adapt to your situation and move closer to accomplishing your life goals."

1. Give me two thoughts you can think that will make you feel better about yourself and your future.
2. Name two places you can go to feel confident about yourself and your future.

3. Now let's work to schedule two times over the course of the next two weeks in which you can go to this place(s) at least one time. (The counselor works with the client to identify a specific date and time in which the client will visit the identified place of empowerment.)
4. Name two people you can talk with to feel confident about yourself and your future.
5. Now let's work to schedule at least one time over the course of the next seven days in which you can go to visit this person. (The counselor works with the client to identify a specific date and time in which the client will visit the identified person of empowerment.)
6. Name two things you can do by yourself to feel confident about yourself and your future.
7. Now let's work to schedule two times over the course of the next two weeks in which you can visit this place. (The counselor works with the client to identify a specific date and time in which he can participate in these empowering activities.)

Desensitize

THERAPIST: "By now you know that life is sometimes crazy, chaotic, and confusing. Life uses people, places, and things to create events that challenge us in our pursuit of success and happiness. If you do not have a psychological defense system in place for handling life stresses, life will overwhelm you and you will begin to think, feel, and behave in negative ways that will not help you accomplish your life goals. What we are going to do now is discuss specifically how you are going to begin to think, feel, and respond to future life challenges. Basically, we are going to develop a strategy that you are going to use to cope, remain balanced, and adapt to future life challenges."

"This strategy will help you to not make bad decisions as a result of emotional discomfort. What we will be doing is identifying the people, places, things, and events that usually upset you and cause you to make bad decisions. We will also be identifying the negative thoughts and emotions you sometimes experience right before you make a bad decision. This psychological defense system will serve as a strategy for controlling your thinking, properly managing your emotions, and channeling your impulses through positive behavior."

1. Cost Benefit Analysis: How can continuing to let your emotions and bad decision-making negatively impact your life?
2. The next time you are feeling emotionally uncomfortable, what can you tell yourself to keep from making a bad decision?
3. Life Skill Role Playing (Mental Rehearsal - Verbal Rehearsal - Behavioral Rehearsal): "Now I want you to imagine telling yourself exactly what you told me you would say the next time you were feeling _______."
4. Now I want you to say what you just imagined yourself saying aloud."
5. I want you to imagine yourself experiencing an uncomfortable emotion. What emotion are you imagining?
6. Give me an example of a positive and productive way in which you can express this emotion.
7. Predetermined Emotion Expression Strategies: "Now I want you to imagine yourself expressing this emotion in the way that you just described."
8. "Do you think that doing and saying the things we have just discussed will keep you from making bad decisions in the future?"
9. Behavior Training Exercises (with self or trusted friend):

"For the next two weeks I want you to continue mentally and verbally rehearsing the strategies and responses we have discussed at home by yourself or with a trusted friend."

Post Session Activity

1. Dream Statement Activity: "At the end of this session I want you to spend 10 minutes outlining how you want your life to look 10 years from now."

2. Dream Statement Visualization: "Now that you have outlined and described your desired future reality, I want you to devote five minutes per day for the next seven days visualizing everything that you have written on this sheet becoming your future reality."

Note: Client should be advised to set a visualization reminder alert on his cell phone.

Therapist Provides Session Summary

SESSION 3

GOAL SETTING

Prior Session Dream Statement Activity Checkpoint

THERAPIST: "The last time we met we talked about some of your life challenges and how they are affecting you mentally and emotionally. Do you feel that your problems have gotten better, worse, or are about the same?" (Note: No matter how the client answers this question, the therapist can still use the same suggested sequence of questioning to address the same problems or a new set of problems.)

Verbalize

1. Have your problems gotten better, worse, or about the same?
2. Why do you think these problems have gotten better, worse, or stayed the same?
3. How have they negatively affected your progression in school, life, and relationships since the last time we met?

Intellectualize

1. What people, places, and things keep this problem alive?
2. What personal role do you play in keeping this problem alive?
3. If this problem is not resolved, how will your life be this time next year?
4. When will you know that this problem has been resolved?

Emotionalize

1. On a scale of 1 to 10, with 1 being "not frustrated at all" and 10 being "overwhelmingly frustrated" how frustrating are your current issues? Explain your response.
2. Does this frustration usually turn into sadness, anger, or both? If so, how often?
3. On scale of 1 to 10, with 1 being "not angry and/or sad at at all" and 10 being "overwhelmingly sad and/or angry" how intense is your anger and/or sadness? Explain your response.
4. How do you usually think and behave when you start to feel this way?
5. In the past, what bad decisions have you made as a result of your emotions of sadness and/or anger?

Spiritualize

1. What have you been learning about life as a result of this problem?
2. If one good thing resulted from this problem, what would it be?

Actualize

1. What future challenges do you think this current problem could be preparing you for?
2. How can this problem make you more effective at achieving future success?
3. What have you gotten better at as a result of this problem?

Utilize

1. How can you use these newfound strengths to overcome your current problems?
2. What can you do more often to make your talents, gifts, and strengths even stronger?

3. What are three goals you want to accomplish in the next 30 days?
4. How are your 30-day goals connected to your long-term vision?
5. Thinking about the goals you have set, how will you use your strengths to accomplish them all?

Stabilize

1. Who can serve as an accountability partner to make sure you are working to accomplish these three goals?
2. When will you contact this person to tell them your goals and explain that you want them to hold you accountable for accomplishing your goals?
3. Now I want you to make a general to-do list of things you need to accomplish over the next two weeks.
4. Now I want you to imagine yourself accomplishing these goals and completing your list of to-dos. How do you feel imagining this success? Do you think you will feel this way when you accomplish these goals and complete your list of to-dos in real life?
5. Deep-Breathing Relaxation Technique: "Now I want you to use deep breathing exercises to manage some of your stress and anxiety. For the next few seconds I want you to take deep slow breaths to naturally calm your mind and body. The way deep relaxation breathing works is like this…first you breathe deeply and slowly through your nose. Next you slowly inhale oxygen through your nose as deeply as you can, hold your breath for a few seconds and then exhale slowly until you have released as much air as you possibly can. While you are using this technique I want you to imagine not only accomplishing your goals but I also want you to imagine experiencing the satisfaction and fulfillment you will experience as a result of accomplishing your goals. Now let's take a few seconds to practice this technique."

Desensitize

1. Thinking about the three personal goals you just told me about, what will you do to make sure you do not allow your weaknesses to keep you from accomplishing the three personal goals you previously mentioned?
2. What will you tell yourself when you feel like your weaknesses are surfacing and negatively influencing your life?
3. Where will you go when you feel like your weaknesses are surfacing and negatively influencing your life?
4. Who will you talk to when you feel like your weaknesses are surfacing and negatively influencing your life?

Post Session Activity

1. Goal Setting Activity: "Before you leave I would like us to spend some time talking about some of your short-term goals and what steps you are planning to take to accomplish these goals." (The therapist should have the client identify three short-term goals and have the client outline the action steps necessary to accomplish the identified goals.)

Therapist Provides Session Summary

SESSION 4

INTERNALIZED STIGMA ASSESSMENT

Prior Session Goal-Setting Activity Checkpoint

Verbalize

THERAPIST: "So let's talk about your life as a Black male living in America. This discussion is important because for whatever reason, Black people encounter different types of racist and discriminatory experiences of which they never really get a chance to sit down and discuss. You and I will be spending the next few sessions not only talking about how racism, stigma, and discrimination can impact your life, but we will also work to create a strategy for using your mental and emotional strengths to overcome racism, stigma, and discrimination situations."

1. Why do you think you are having so much trouble doing well in school and staying out of trouble? (If applicable)
2. Do you ever feel like giving up on school? (If therapist feels is applicable)
3. Do you think you can graduate high school, graduate college, get a good job, and achieve the American Dream?
4. Why do you think you have made bad decisions in recent times?
5. Give me an example of a time when stress, sadness, fear, or frustration caused you to make a bad decision. What bad decision did you make?
6. Why do you think Black males struggle to be successful in America?
7. Do you think people in society respect and value you as a Black?

8. Do you ever believe some of the negative messages and stereotypes about Black males?
9. Have you ever heard of Internalized Stigma? Internalized Stigma is when a person starts to believe and accept the negative messages that other people may say or think about them.
10. Thinking about who you are as a person and some of the bad decisions you have made in the past, do you think you have internalized some of the negative messages society spreads about Black males? If so, what negative messages about Black males are you struggling not to believe to be true about yourself?

Intellectualize

THERAPIST: "There are a lot of crazy things going on in the country as it relates to racism. Let's take some time to really think deeply about how racism, stigma, and discrimination may be negatively impacting your life. Sometimes racism can create issues for Black males and sometimes Black males create issues for themselves. We are going to use our brains to work together to develop a strategy that will help you overcome the things within yourself and within your environment that cause the problems you sometimes have in life."

1. How do you personally define racism?
2. Do you see the world as fair?
3. How many times a day do you think about the fact that America is not fair?
4. What if you lived in a world where everything was fair; what would be different about your life?
5. If everything was equal for all people would you have the problem(s) that you have now?
6. What similarities do you see in the problems you are having and the problems that other people like you have in this country?
7. Why do you think these similarities exist?

8. Who did you see struggling with racism when you were growing up?
9. How did seeing their struggles affect how you see America?
10. What issues did your family or other people you know have as a result of racism?
11. What did you learn about racism from your family, friends, and associates?
12. How did they teach you to respond to racism?
13. Do you think the media mainly shows negative images of Black males? Explain your answer.

Emotionalize

THERAPIST: "I am sure you are experiencing various thoughts and emotions about racism and your life in America. We all know guys are trained to not express emotions and feelings about the things in life that are troubling them. As human beings however, it is important that you can acknowledge not only how you see, interpret, and understand your experiences with racism and stigma, but it is also important to come to grips with how these issues have emotionally impacted you as it relates to the fear, frustration, sadness, and anger that you are experiencing as a result of your experiences with racism, stigma, and discrimination. So, let's spend some time talking about how you feel about your life as a Black male in America."

1. What have been your worst experiences of racism?
2. How do these experiences affect how you see yourself, your life, and your future?
3. How would you describe your experience as a Black male in America?
4. What do you feel is America's overriding message to Black males?
5. Do you feel like America values you as a Black male?
6. Express to me the sadness or frustration that you sometimes feel as a Black male in America.

7. How do you typically respond to negative messages about Black males?
8. When you feel like America is giving you a bad message about who you are and what your future holds, how do you respond emotionally?
9. How do you keep from believing the negative messages about yourself and your future?
10. Are any of your self-esteem issues related to how you feel America perceives you as a Black male?

Post Session Activity

Stigma Awareness and Aversion Activities

1. *Inspirational Movie Viewing:* Client and therapist should work to identify one to three Black American themed movies. The purpose of this activity is to provide the Black male client with theatrical role-models who can inspire him and provide observable instructions on how to maintain dignity, self-respect, and cultural pride in the face of racism.

2. *Artistic Expression Activities:* For this activity, the client will have the option of using the creative arts (e.g. poetry, journaling, drawing, painting, hip-hop, etc.) to serve as a healthy outlet for expressing his thoughts and feelings as it relates to his concerns about racism. This activity will provide the client with an opportunity to express his personal commitment to not internalize stigma and to not become a statistic.

3. *Stigma Response Script:* This activity will require the client to develop a response script (mental, verbal, and behavioral) that he will use when encountering stigmatic messages and racist interactions. This script can be internal (how he will mentally frame, interpret, and respond to stigma) and/or external (what behaviors he will utilize to navigate racism).

Therapist Provides a Session Summary

SESSION 5

MAKING THE CONNECTION: INTERNALIZED STIGMA AND BAD DECISION MAKING

Prior Session Stigma Awareness and Aversion Activity Checkpoint

THERAPIST: "As we talked about before, internalized stigma is when a person starts to believe and accept the negative messages other people may say or think about them."

Verbalize

1. Based upon the definition I just gave you how would you define internalized stigma?
2. What are your thoughts about the concept of internalized stigma?

Intellectualize (Internalized Stigma)

1. Why is it important that you not allow yourself to internalize negative messages about Black males?
2. What negative messages about Black males do you sometimes believe or identify with?
3. Why do you think you sometimes believe that these messages are true of who you are as a Black male?
4. What negative messages about your future as a Black male do you sometimes believe?
5. Why do you think it is hard to not believe this to be true about your future?
6. Are any of your self-esteem issues related to how you feel America perceives you as a Black male?
7. What part of the task of not internalizing racism seems to be the hardest or most out of your control?

8. What part of the task of not internalizing racism seems to be totally in your control?

Intellectualize: The Connection between Internalized Stigma and Bad Decision-Making

1. Why do you think you have made some bad decisions in recent times?
2. Give me an example of a time when stress, sadness, fear, or frustration caused you to make a bad decision. What bad decision did you make?
3. Thinking about who you are as a person and some of the decisions you make, do you think you have internalized some of society's messages about Black males? If so, what negative messages about Black males are you struggling to not believe to be true about yourself?
4. Do you think your bad decision-making is related to you having internalized the stigma surrounding Black males?
5. What usually triggers you to engage in bad decision-making?
6. When you are in the process of making a bad decision, are you aware that the decision you are making is a poor decision?
7. How has your bad decision-making negatively influenced your life?
8. What parts of your behavior do you feel are the result of you behaving as Black males are stereotyped to behave?
9. What is the most difficult part about stopping yourself from behaving like a Black male who has internalized racism?

Emotionalize

1. When you feel like America is giving you a bad message about who you are and what your future holds, how do you respond emotionally?
2. What part of this task of not internalizing racism seems to be most frustrating for you?
3. Do you ever feel angry about the fact that you have to deal with these negative messages?
4. How do you deal with this anger?
5. Do you ever feel sad about the fact that you have to protect yourself from internalizing negative messages?
6. How do you deal with this sadness?
7. Have your emotions surrounding racism ever caused you to make bad decisions?
8. Give me two examples of when these emotions caused you to make a bad decision.
9. How did you feel after you made these decisions?
10. How are you feeling right now as we talk about not internalizing racism?
11. Usually when you think or talk about the reality of racism, how do you feel?
12. How would you prefer to feel when you think about or talk about racism?

Post Session Activity

Stigma Processing and Bad-Decision Making Prevention Activities:

Stigma Processing and Reconditioning

1. *Thought and Message Replacement Activity:* On the left side of the sheet provided make a list of the negative messages society says about Black males. On the right side of the sheet make a list of positive messages you will begin to say about yourself.

Behavioral Reconditioning Activity

1. *Personifying Racism Journal Activity:* The client should be given a handout that includes instructions to journal a response to the items below:

    a. Finish this sentence: Now that I know racism has the deliberate goal of causing me to doubt my potential and not believe in myself, I have decided to __________.

    b. I want you to finish this sentence: Now that I know racism and stigma have the goal causing me to make decisions that will hurt my life and my future success, I have decided not to __________.

    c. If racism were a person what would you say to him or her?

    d. What do you think racism would say back to you?

    e. What would you say in response?

    f. Do you believe in the power of your response? Please explain.

Therapist Provides Session Summary

SESSION 6

FEAR OF FAILURE, MANHOOD, & FATHER FORGIVENESS

(If applicable to the client's life-story)

Note: The topic of forgiveness may need to be addressed for two sessions if the client has resentment towards his father as well as other individuals. In contrast, if the client does not have resentment issues towards his father the questions and assignments related to forgiving his father can be skipped over.

Prior Session Stigma Processing and Bad-Decision Making Activity Checkpoint

THERAPIST: "How would you describe your relationship with your biological father? Based upon what you just told me, I am assuming you feel as if your father has not truly been there for you. For whatever reason, a great number of Black children do not live with their biological fathers. Sometimes children who do not have a father in their life feel as if they have missed out on certain things in life. There is no doubt that there are a lot of emotions, stress, and pain that comes with the burden of not having your father around."

"Resentment and unforgiveness are two common emotions a person may have towards an absentee or emotionally unavailable father. Resentment and unforgiveness can cause a person to not live freely and fully. This lack of freedom can cause a person to live a life of frustration, anger, and sadness. Today we are going to talk about what thoughts and feelings of unforgiveness you may have towards your father. We will also be talking about how you will go about forgiving your father for not truly being in your life."

Fear of Failure

Verbalize

1. What are your career goals?
2. Do you feel you have power over your future?

Intellectualizing

1. Do you feel like your problems are related to your sense of not having control over your life?
2. What usually causes you to want to give up on your life goals?
3. Do you ever fear that you will fail to accomplish your life goals?
4. How often do you think about your fears?
5. What do you fear most about your future?
6. Are any aspects of your fear of failure a result of your concerns about the impact that racism may have on your future?
7. Some of the behaviors that you have manifested are typical of an individual who has internalized stigma. Thinking about some of your bad decision-making in the past, do you think it has anything to do with the fact that you may be starting to believe what society says about your future as a Black male?
8. Are any of your behaviors related to trying to escape the fear of failure?
9. What do you feel can cause you to fail?
10. What are some bad things you imagine happening to you if you were to fail?
11. Is this fear of failure affecting your focus and motivation?

12. What have you been doing to cope with your fear of failure?
13. What else could you do to cope more effectively with your fear of failure?
14. What parts of yourself can stop you from becoming the person you want to be?
15. What do you feel lack at as it relates to having what it takes to be successful?
16. What specific life experiences caused you to have the fears you have now?

THERAPIST: "We have discussed life challenges, increasing your self-esteem, and accomplishing your life goals. In our last two meetings we talked about building healthy relationships and managing stress. Sometimes it can be hard being or becoming a man. There are a lot of roles, rules, and responsibilities of manhood that you may never fully understand unless somebody tells you. This can cause a lot of confusion and frustration. Today we are going to talk about what manhood means to you and specifically what you need to do to become the man you desire to be."

Manhood

Verbalize

1. How do you define a "Real Man?

Intellectualize

1. Who do you consider to be a "Real Man"?
2. What qualities about this person make him a "Real Man"?
3. Do you consider your father a "Real Man"?
4. What did your father teach you about manhood?
5. How would you describe your relationship with your father?
6. Do you ever feel like not having a father around has caused you to be unaware of things you should know?

7. Are there some topics about life and manhood that you feel you you lack understanding?
8. Where did you get the information on manhood you have now?
9. Did you ever feel vulnerable or unprotected because your father was rarely around?
10. Do you ever feel like you had to become a man way too early in order to help your family because of your father not being around?
11. Do you trust men in general? Why or why not?

Emotionalize

1. Do you ever feel like you missed out on certain things because your father was rarely around?
2. How often do you think about the fact that your father was not in your life?
3. What usually causes you to think about the fact that your father was not in your life the way you feel he should have been?
4. What was the most frustrating part of not having your father around?
5. Do you feel mostly angry or mostly sad about your father not being in your life? Please explain.
6. How do you handle these emotion?

Spiritualize

1. Did you learn any life lessons about manhood as a result of your father's weaknesses or issues?
2. Do you ever feel special knowing that your only father figure has been that of your Higher Power?
3. Assuming that praying for someone who has hurt you can help you to forgive them, how often do you pray for your father?

4. What are some positive things that have occurred due to your father not being around?
5. Can you think of any negative outcomes that may have occurred if your father would have been in your life?
6. How can your Higher Power help you to view your father in a more positive light?

Actualize

1. You obviously have made it this far despite not having a father in your life. In what ways are you proud of yourself for what you have accomplished as a young man despite not having a father there to help you?
2. What are some strengths you have developed as a result of not having a father figure?
3. What positive things about you, and who you are as a man, are the result of not having a father around and having to take on responsibilities at such an early age?

Utilize

1. Has not having your father around during childhood motivated you to be in the lives of your future children? Please explain.
2. Do you ever see yourself helping other young men who have not had a father in their life? If so, in what ways can you help young men struggling with fatherlessness?
3. What is the greatest lesson you can teach these young men about becoming a "Real Man"?

Stabilize

1. Do you feel like you need to forgive your father for not being in your life?
2. For what, specifically, do you need to forgive him?
3. If he were sitting in this room right now what would you say to him?

Desensitize

1. Help client develop a list of three reasons why he should forgive his father.
2. Help client develop a prayer or list of positive words about his father he can recite to substitute the negative thoughts he many have towards his father.
3. Help the client develop a list of three excuses or merciful explanations for why their father did what he did to hurt him. (Examples: 1. “My father was very young when he had me. He must have been terrified by the thought of taking care of another life and maybe that is why he ran from his responsibilities.” 2. “My father’s father was not there for him so I could see how my dad would repeat his father’s mistakes as there was no one in his life to teach him how to be a “Real Man” and a good father.” 3. “My father was heavy into drugs and I could see how his addictions could have caused him to lose his way and not be mentally or emotionally available to his child.”)

   “This does not mean what my father did was not wrong, it just means that I understand how a person who was had these types of experiences could turn out to be an uninvolved father.”

Post Session Activity

I. *Fear Confrontation Activity*

1. What are some fears and concerns you have about your future as a result of racism?
2. What can you do to protect yourself from allowing these fears to become your reality?
3. In what areas of life do you fear failure?
4. What will you do to protect your confidence and self-esteem despite these fears?

5. Who do you know that seems to have conquered racism in America?
6. What can you learn from this person?
7. What do you think this person would say if you asked him to mentor you on how to achieve success in America?

II. *No Fear Visualization Activity*

1. "For the next seven days, I want you to set aside three minutes a day visualizing success. I want you to sit in a quiet place with your eyes closed while listening to motivational music in the background. Focus on controlling yourself in class. Focus on passing your classes. Focus on graduating from high school. Focus on going to college. Focus on graduating from college and making your loved ones proud and proving everyone who did not believe in you that they were wrong! I also want you to focus on getting a great job and having the things you want in your future."

III. *Father Forgiveness Activities*

1. *Thought Replacement Activity:* "Your post session activity will be to build a process that will help you forgive your father for the disappointment he has brought you. On the left side of a sheet of paper list some of the negative thoughts

   you have about your father. Now on the right side of the paper write down positive thoughts to replace the negative thoughts you have listed about your father."

2. *Letter Writing and Burning Exercise (option #1):* "For this exercise you will write a letter to your father. You will be explaining to your father the things he has done to disappoint you, how what he has done has impacted your life, and why you have chosen to forgive him for his shortcomings. After you have written the letter you will bring it to our next

session and read it to me. After you have read it to me you will burn the letter in symbolism of putting the past behind you."

Letter Writing and Delivery Exercise (option #2): "For this exercise you will write a letter to your father. You will explain to your father what he did to hurt you, how what he did to you has impacted your life and why you have chosen to forgive him. After you have written the letter you will bring it to our next session and read it to me. After you have read it to me you will then determine a time in which you will deliver the letter to your father. You can choose to have your father read the letter in your presence or you can choose to mail the letter to your father."

3. *Creative Expression:* In this exercise, the client can be presented with the opportunity to use his creative ability to produce an artistic piece that symbolizes his pursuit of forgiveness towards his father. Producing a poem or song about forgiveness or drawing/painting a picture symbolizing forgiveness can be a very productive method for channeling emotions and fostering forgiveness.

4. *Positive Visualization Exercise:* For this exercise the client should be instructed to visualize himself forgiving his father. By instructing the client to imagine saying, "I forgive you", hugging his father, or just smiling at his father, the client is psychologically preparing himself to gradually forgive his father and move on with his life.

Therapist Provides Session Summary

SESSION 7

FORGIVING & MOVING ON: HEALING FROM PAST RELATIONSHIPS

Prior Session Fear of Failure and Father Forgiveness Activity Checkpoint

THERAPIST: "So, we have discussed life challenges, racism, the fear of failure, manhood, and forgiving your father for his shortcomings. Throughout life you will come across people who will hurt and/or wrong you. Sometimes it can be hard living a full life when we have people in our lives whom we have not forgiven. There are a lot of emotions, stress, and pain that come with the burden of not letting go and forgiving. These painful emotions can cause us to not live freely and fully. This lack of freedom can cause us to live lives of frustration, anger, and sadness. Today we are going to be talking about what forgiveness means to you, who you need to forgive and how you will go about forgiving this person(s)."

Verbalize

1. How do you define "forgiveness?"

Intellectualize

1. Who do you feel you need to forgive?
2. Do you believe this person deserves your forgiveness?
3. What did this person do to hurt or wrong you?
4. How would you describe your current relationship with this person?

5. Do you ever feel like not forgiving this person will hurt you more than forgiving this person?
6. How has this person affected you as it relates to your other relationships?

Emotionalize

1. Do you ever feel like this person has stolen something from you as it relates to who you are as a person?
2. How often do you think about the fact that this person has hurt or wronged you?
3. What was the most frustrating or hurtful part of what this person did to you?
4. Do you feel mostly angry or mostly sad when you think about this person and what they did to you?
5. How do you handle these emotions?

Spiritualize

1. Did you learn any life lessons because of this person's actions?
2. Assuming that praying for someone can help you forgive him or her, how often do you pray for this person?
3. What, if any, are some positive things that came out of this situation?

Actualize

1. You obviously have made it this far despite this person doing what they have done to you. In what ways are you proud of yourself for what you have accomplished as a person despite the pain that this person has brought into your life?
2. What are some strengths you have developed because of this life experience?

3. What positive things about you as a person are the results of having this negative experience with this particular person?

Utilize

1. Has the way this person treated you motivated you to treat people as best you can? Explain your answer.
2. Do you ever see yourself helping other people who were wronged in a similar way you were wronged?
3. What is the greatest lesson you can teach others about how to forgive people who have hurt them?

Stabilize

1. What specifically do you need to forgive this person for doing?
2. Empty Chair Technique: If this person were sitting in this room right now what would you say to them?

Desensitize

1. Help client develop a list of three reasons why he should forgive this person.
2. Help client develop a prayer or list of positive words about this person that he can recite to substitute the negative thoughts he many have towards this person.
3. Help client develop a list of three excuses or merciful explanations for why the person did what they did to hurt them. (Example: "My step-father was very wrong for molesting me, however he was molested as a child by his father so I could see how he could become a molester himself. This does not mean what he did was not terribly wrong; it just means I understand how a person who was molested could then themselves become a child molester.")

Post Session Activity

1. Forgiveness Activity: "We are now going to spend the next few minutes building a process that will help you forgive this person for what they have done to you."

2. Letter Writing and Burning Exercise (option #1): "For this exercise you will write a letter to the person you need to forgive. You will be explaining to the person what they did to hurt you, how what they did to you has impacted your life, and why you have chosen to forgive them. After you have written the letter you will bring it to our next session and read it to me. After you have read it to me you will burn the letter in symbolism of putting the past behind you."

3. Letter Writing and Delivery Exercise (option #2): "For this exercise you will write a letter to the person you need to forgive. You will be explaining to the person what they did to hurt you, how what they did to you has impacted your life, and why you have chosen to forgive them. After you have written the letter you will bring it to our next session and read it to me. After you have read it to me you will then determine a time in which you will deliver the letter to the person you are working to forgive. You can choose to have the person read the letter in your presence or mail the letter to the individual."

4. Creative Expression: In this exercise, the client can be presented with the opportunity to use his creative ability to produce an artistic piece that symbolizes their pursuit of forgiveness. Producing a poem or song about forgiveness or drawing/painting a picture symbolizing forgiveness can be a very productive method for channeling emotions and fostering forgiveness.

5. Positive Visualization Exercise: For this exercise the client should be instructed to visualize themselves forgiving the

person who has hurt them. By instructing the client to imagine saying "I forgive you", hugging the person, or just smiling at the person they need to forgive, the client is psychologically preparing themselves to forgive the person they are having trouble forgiving.

Therapist Provides Session Summary

SESSION 8

PROCESSING THE BLACK EXPERIENCE

Prior Session Father Forgiveness and/or General Forgiveness Activity Checkpoint

THERAPIST: “Using the philosophy or logic that assumes everything happens for a reason and everything has some type of purpose, let's work to discover the meaning or the reason for why Black people have had such a hard time in America. When you find meaning, purpose, and positive messages in hard times, you are more likely to be able to cope with and overcome your situations. Furthermore, you are less likely to feel weak, vulnerable, and powerless to the things that are trying to sabotage your progress. For the next few minutes we are going to work together to find meaning, purpose, and positivity in not only your struggles as a Black male but also in the struggles of Black people as a whole.”

Spiritualize

1. In the big picture of life why do you think Blacks have been discriminated against for so long?
2. What are two great things that can come from the struggles Black people have historically experienced in America?
3. How has the Black struggle influenced your perception of life?
4. How has your Higher Power helped you handle living in a racist society?
5. How will the successful accomplishing of your life goals benefit you emotionally?
6. How will the successful accomplishing of your life goals

benefit your children?

7. How will the successful accomplishing of your life goals benefit other Black Americans?
8. How will the successful accomplishing of your life goals bring validation to your religion and/or Higher Power?

Actualize

THERAPIST: "Have you ever heard the saying 'that which does not kill you only makes you stronger? If that is true, then Black people should be the strongest race on the planet as they have had to endure hardships around the world for thousands of years. It is very important that you do not let experiences of racism, stigma, and discrimination make you weak and vulnerable. It is important that you learn how to use racism as a motivator for hard work and success. For the next few minutes we will be talking about the knowledge, strengths, and abilities you have acquired as a result of your experiences with racism, stigma, and discrimination."

1. As a people, what do you consider the two greatest things about Black Americans?
2. What are the cultural strengths of Black Americans?
3. What can other races learn from Black Americans?
4. Are you proud to be Black? Why or why not?
5. What do you like most about being Black?
6. What specific strengths do you think you have acquired as a result of being a Black male living in a racist society?

Utilize

THERAPIST: "Now that we have identified the strengths, talents, abilities, and skills that your experiences with racism have brought you, let's talk about ways in which you can use these strengths to protect yourself from internalizing the negative messages that society spreads about Black males. Also, let's discuss how your strengths can be used as a means of overcoming some of your other life issues that we have not discussed."

1. What do you think it will take for you to not internalize racism when you experience it in the future?
2. How can you use your personal struggles to help other Blacks conquer racism, stigma, and discrimination?
3. What can you do to improve the overall Black experience in America?
4. As it relates to respecting and honoring the great accomplishments of past Black Americans, what responsibility do you have to be successful?

Stabilize

THERAPIST: "Okay, so we have talked about how racism, stigma, and discrimination have impacted your life. We have also talked about your feelings surrounding racism and have also worked to find meaning and purpose in your experiences of racism and stigma. Finally, we have identified some of the strengths you have acquired as a result of your experiences with stigma and discrimination and how you can use these strengths to overcome your current and future life challenges."

"Now let's talk about how you are going to not only mentally and emotionally respond to negative messages about Black males but also how you are going to successfully cope and productively respond to racism. Essentially, we will work to develop a strategy for achieving a level of mental and emotional adaption that allows you to sustain productive functioning even when you are facing extreme forms of racism, stigma, and discrimination. Let's take a few minutes to discuss a few strategies you can use to overcome racism and protect yourself from believing and accepting negative messages about Black males."

1. What can you do to remind yourself not to allow racist messages to affect how you view yourself and your future?
2. What usually triggers you to engage in bad decision-making?
3. What three people can help you effectively manage your life and your reality?
4. What organization or community resource can you use to manage your life and your reality more effectively?

Desensitize

THERAPIST: "By now you know that as a Black male you may potentially encounter racism and discrimination. By now you also have noticed that a lot of messages about Black males in society are negative. If you do not have a psychological defense system in place, racism, stigma, and discrimination can discourage you and cause you to doubt yourself and your future. If you do not have a psychological defense system in place to protect yourself from believing these negative messages, you will begin to think, feel, and behave in ways that will not help you accomplish your life goals."

"What we are going to do now is discuss specifically how you are going to begin to think, feel, and respond to future challenges with racism. Basically, we are going to develop a strategy that you are going to use to cope with future race-related challenges. This strategy will help keep you from making bad decisions because of the emotional discomfort you may sometimes feel because of your experiences with racism. What we will do is identify the types of negative messages about you and your future you sometimes have trouble not believing. We will also identify the negative thoughts and emotions you sometimes experience right before you make a bad decision. This psychological defense system will serve as a strategy for controlling your thinking, properly managing your emotions, and channeling your impulses through positive behavior."

1. Why is important that you not allow yourself to internalize the negative messages out there about Black males?
2. What negative messages about Black males do you sometimes believe or identify with?
3. Why do you think you sometimes believe that these messages are true of who you are as a Black male?
4. What negative messages about your future as a Black male do you sometimes have trouble not believing and accepting?
5. Why do you think it is hard not to believe this to be true about your future?
6. What are two positive things you can tell yourself when you are feeling unappreciated by American society?
7. What are two positive things you can tell yourself you when find yourself doubting your ability to accomplish your life goals?
8. When you are feeling angry, what are three productive ways in which you can express your anger?
9. When you are feeling sad, what are three productive ways in which you can express your sadness?
10. What can you do in the next 24 hours to start thinking more positively about who you are as a Black male?
11. What can you do in the next 24 hours to start thinking more positively about your future as a Black man?
12. Name two people who make you feel bad about yourself and your future. What steps will you take in the next 24 hours to eliminate or minimize contact with these people?
13. Name two people who make you feel good about yourself and your future. What steps will you take in the next 24 hours to spend time with these people?

Post Session Activity

Strength Finding Activity

1. Why do you think you were created a Black male?
2. List three reasons why you are proud to be a Black male.
3. What is the best part about being a Black male?
4. How has your Higher Power helped you handle living in a racist society?
5. List three specific strengths you have as a result of being a Black male living in a racist society.
6. List three ways in which you can use these personal strengths to protect yourself from internalizing negative messages about who you are as a Black male.

Meaning-Making Activity

1. How will successfully accomplishing your life goals benefit your children or future children?
2. List three other people who will benefit from your future success.
3. How will successfully accomplishing your life goals bring validation to your religion or Higher Power?
4. How can you use your personal struggles to help other Blacks conquer racism, stigma, and discrimination?

Therapist Provides Session Summary

SESSION 9

STRATEGICALLY AND SUCCESSFULLY COPING WITH RACISM AND DISCRIMINATION

Prior Session Strength-Finding and Meaning-Making Activity Checkpoint

THERAPIST: "Today we are going talk about productive ways of mentally and emotionally responding to negative messages about Black males. Today we will also discuss how you are going to successfully cope with racism and respond to it in a way that benefits your life. Essentially, we will be working to develop a strategy for achieving a level of mental and emotional adaption that allows you to sustain productive functioning even when you are facing extreme forms of racism, stigma, and discrimination. Let's take a few minutes to discuss strategies you can use to overcome racism and protect yourself from believing and accepting the negative messages about Black Males."

Verbalize

1. Describe how racism has impacted your life thus far.
2. What proof do you have that racism has negatively impacted your life?
3. Why do you think there is so much racism in America?
4. When did you first realize that you were living in a country that is racist towards Black males?
5. Why do you think racism exists?
6. How often do you think about racism?
7. How do you feel when you think about racism?
8. What do you do to deal with the stress, strain, and frustration of racism?
9. Why do you think you respond in this manner?

10. How are your thoughts about yourself affected by your experiences with racism?
11. How are your thoughts about your life and your future affected by your experiences with racism?

Intellectualize

1. Why do you think Black males have so much trouble achieving success in America?
2. What usually triggers you to engage in bad decision-making?
3. When you are in the process of making a bad decision, do you know that the decision you are making is a poor decision?
4. How has your decision-making negatively affected your life?
5. What parts of your behavior do you feel are the result of you behaving as Black males are stereotyped to behave?

Emotionalize

1. Let us assume that for whatever reason, sometimes you feel saddened, angered, and frustrated about how Black males are stereotyped and treated in America. How do you deal with these emotions?
2. What are some productive ways in which you will express the uncomfortable emotions you feel when you think about living in an unfair world?

Spiritualize

1. If you were God what would you like most about Black people?
2. If you were God what would you like most about you?
3. If you were God what would you say to you when you are feeling bad about yourself and your future?

Actualize

1. What three personal strengths can help you effectively protect yourself from internalizing negative messages about Black males?
2. What will you do to protect your confidence and self-esteem despite the negative messages about Black males you see, hear, and experience?
3. What is your plan for not internalizing negative messages about who you are as a Black male?

Utilize

1. Thinking about some of your concerns about the ability of racism to negatively influence your future, what can you do to protect yourself from racism?
2. When you are not feeling good about who you are as a Black male in America, what can you tell yourself to feel better and think more positively?
3. Is there anyone you can talk to who you feel can give you good advice on how to overcome racism?

Stabilize

1. What will you do to change behaviors that will not help you accomplish your life goals?
2. What can you do to remind yourself not to allow racist messages to affect how you view yourself and your future?
3. What will you do to think positive thoughts about yourself and your future?
4. What will you do to think positive thoughts about other Black males?
5. What can you do to make sure that you are not racist towards other Black males?

Desensitize

1. What two people can you spend more time with in order to remain positive, make good decisions, and not internalize negative messages about Black males?
2. What organization or community resource can you access in order to remain positive, make good decisions, and not internalize negative messages about Black males?

Post Session Activity

1. *Stigma Response Script:* This activity will require the client to develop a response script (mental, verbal, and behavioral) that he will use when encountering stigmatic messages and racist interactions. This script can be internal (how he will mentally frame, interpret, and respond to stigma) and/or external (what behaviors he will utilize to navigate racism).

Therapist Provides Session Summary

SESSION 10

LIFE MANAGEMENT STRATEGY & TRIGGER DESENSITIZATION PLAN

Prior Session Coping with Racism and Discrimination Activity Checkpoint

General Life Progress Checkpoint

THERAPIST: "As a Black male, it is very important that you have a thorough understanding of how negative messages about Black males impact your thoughts, emotions, and behaviors. It is also important that you know exactly to what degree, if any, you have begun to believe these messages about yourself and your future. This understanding will help you maintain control over your perceptions, emotions, and behavior. This control will increase your ability to accomplish your life goals. Today we are going to work together to build a strategy for developing a positive identity, managing emotions, overcoming racism, protecting your self-esteem, accomplishing your goals, and becoming the man you desire to be."

Verbalize

1. How has internalized stigma served as a barrier to your achievement of a successful life?
2. How has internalized stigma affected your behavior and decision-making?
3. What habits, weaknesses, and behaviors have you been engaging in that are potentially a reflection of you slowly beginning to accept and believe the negative messages about Black males?

Intellectualize

1. Why do you think you have begun to accept these negative messages about Black males?
2. What usually happens to cause you to feel like these negative messages about you and your future are true?
3. What would you say caused you to make the last bad decision you made?
4. What thoughts are you usually thinking right before you make a bad decision?

Emotionalize

1. When you make bad decisions how does it make you feel?
2. Explain to me the disappointment you predict experiencing if you do not accomplish your life goals.
3. Are there any people in your life who would be disappointed if you failed to accomplish your life goals?

Spiritualize

1. What will be the consequences for your family if you do not successfully complete your life goals?
2. Does your religion teach that there are eternal rewards if you make good decisions and accomplish your life goals?
3. For the sake of humankind, do you feel like it is an obligation for you to be successful? Why or why not?

Actualize

1. In what area of life do you fear failure?
2. What will you do to protect your confidence and self-esteem despite the negative messages you see, hear, and experience?
3. What will you do to think positive thoughts about yourself and your future?

4. What are some productive ways in which you will express your emotions?
5. What negative people will you avoid in order to stay focused on your life goals?
6. What people will you spend more quality time around in order to stay focused on your life goals?
7. What strategies will you use to manage future stress?

Utilize

1. What three personal strengths can help you effectively manage your life and your reality?
2. What three people can help you effectively manage your life and your reality?
3. What organization or community resource can you use to manage your life and your reality more effectively?

Stabilize

1. What can you do to remind yourself of the future consequences when you feel like making a bad decision?
2. Are there any places you plan to stop going in order to increase your chance at success?
3. Allow client to rehearse overcoming situations that typically trigger bad decision-making (i.e. have the client to practice desired response in his head or with therapist).
4. Help client develop a system of thinking that will improve his decision-making ability (e.g. cost-benefit analysis).

Desensitize

1. External Threats Identification and Avoidance Strategy: The client and the therapist will work to identify the people, places, and things that negatively impact his decision-making. These negative people, places, and things should be either entered into the client's cell phone or handwritten for future referencing. Once the list has been generated, the client and

therapist will discuss strategies for avoiding these people, places, and things.

2. Avoidance Strategy Visualization and Rehearsal: Once the strategies for avoiding the identified negative people, places, and things has been outlined, the client will visualize himself practicing the outlined strategies. Once he has visualized himself utilizing these strategies he will practice the various strategies with the counselor. For example, the client may develop a response script as a strategy for not giving in to the temptation to skip school with his friends. The therapist will role-play the client's friend who usually ask him to skip school. The client will practice his developed response script with the therapist.

Post Session Activity

1. Trigger Prevention Strategy: The therapist and client will develop a strategy using some of the suggested trigger alleviation strategies listed earlier in this section of the book. This trigger alleviation plan will serve as a psychological defense system that will protect the client from relapsing into counterproductive psychological functioning.

** From this point forward the focus of therapy sessions shift from stigma internalization to general life challenges and issues. The therapist should still make an intentional effort to regularly evaluate, modify, and practice the client's established strategy for not internalizing racism. This strategy reviewing and modification process serves the purpose of continuously increasing a Black male client's ability to not allow internalized racism and social discrimination to trigger failure in the other areas of his complex life.*

SESSION 11

SELF-EFFICACY & SELF-ESTEEM

Prior Session Life Management and Trigger Desensitization Activity Checkpoint

THERAPIST: "In past sessions we have talked about some of your life challenges and how they were affecting you mentally and emotionally. We also talked about accomplishing your life goals. Since the last time we met do you feel your life in general has become better, worse, or stayed about the same?" (Note: No matter how the client answers this question the therapist can still use the same suggested sequence of questioning to address the same problems or a new set of problems.)

Verbalize

1. If you could change one thing about your life what would it be?
2. What makes this part of your life so uncomfortable?
3. Who or what created this problem?

Intellectualize

1. What specific part of your problem has gotten better as of late?
2. Why do you think this part has gotten better?
3. What specifically about your problem has gotten worse as of late?
4. Why do you think this part has gotten worse?
5. What specific part of your problem has stayed the same?
6. Does this problem affect how you see yourself as a person? Why or why not?

7. Does any part of this current problem make you feel bad about yourself? Why or why not?
8. What are your two most frequent negative thoughts about yourself?
9. How often do you have these thoughts?

Emotionalize

1. What usually causes you to have these negative thoughts about yourself?
2. How do these negative thoughts about yourself affect you emotionally?
3. How do you think these thoughts about yourself can affect your everyday decision-making?
4. How have you been emotionally dealing with the negative thoughts you have been having about yourself and your life because of this situation?

Spiritualize

1. Who has the greatest influence on how you view yourself?
2. If you were made in the image of your Higher Power, in what ways would you two be similar?
3. In the big picture of your life what are your two greatest accomplishments?

Actualize

1. What are two good things people say about you?
2. Thinking about the negative thoughts you have about yourself, what two positive thoughts can you replace these negative thoughts with?
3. What are two things you can commit to doing for the next 30 days that will help you focus on your strengths and increase your self-esteem?

Utilize

1. What are two things you consider yourself to be good at?
2. Where in the community can you serve as a volunteer?
3. Do you have any family, friends, or associates that could use your help with a current life problem?

Stabilize

1. What person or group of people make you feel good about yourself?
2. What person or group of people make you feel bad about yourself?
3. Who do you most often compare yourself to? Does this comparison help/motivate or hurt/demotivate you?
4. What can you do to stop making these demotivating harmful comparisons?

Desensitize

1. Name two positive people you can be around to make yourself feel good about who you are.
2. Name one positive place you can go to feel good about yourself and your future.

Post Session Activity

Positive Statement Activity (past, present, and future)

"Now I would like for you to write down seven positive self-statements you will say aloud two times per day for the next seven days." The client should be instructed to type these statements into his phone and set two alert times that will remind him to read and/or say his list of positive affirmations.

Example Self-Affirmation Statements

Past

1. It is not my fault that someone took advantage of me when I was younger…there was nothing I could do!
2. I forgive myself for the mistakes I have made in the past…nobody is perfect!
3. I forgive everyone who has ever hurt me!

Present

1. I am a smart person!
2. I am a brave person!
3. Good people like and respect me!
4. I can do all things through God who strengthens me!

Future

1. I will graduate high school, graduate college, and get a great job!
2. I will live a long and happy life!
3. I will be a successful person!

Therapist Provides Session Summary

SESSION 12

BUILDING HEALTHY RELATIONSHIPS

Prior Session Self-Efficacy and Self-Esteem Activity Checkpoint

THERAPIST: "Over the course of the last few months we have discussed many topics related to achieving life success and life happiness. Today we will talk a little deeper about those topics but we will also be spending time talking about the people in your life. So let's get started!"

Verbalize

1. As it relates to the fear of failure, self-esteem, and emotional management, in what areas do you feel you are making the most progress?
2. As it relates to the fear of failure, self-esteem, and emotional management, in what areas do you feel you are making the least progress?

Intellectualize

1. Why do think you are making the most progress in the area of ____?
2. Why do you think you are making the least amount of progress in the area of ____?
3. Who makes it harder for you to change your life?
4. In what ways do these people negatively influence your life?
5. Why do you think you still interact with these people even though they have a negative influence on your life?

Emotionalize

1. Do you ever fear rejection and/or loneliness?

2. How do these fears make you feel emotionally?
3. Have you ever made a bad decision or put yourself in a bad position because of the fear of rejection and loneliness?
4. Do you think there are any fears or emotions that play a part in your decision to continue to interact with these people?

Spiritualize

1. Life often uses people to challenge us and teach us life lessons. Why do you think these people are in your life?
2. What have you learned about people because of these negative relationships?
3. Do you feel like you have a good or meaningful relationship with a Higher Power?
4. How does this relationship with your Higher Power help you more effectively live life?
5. How can improving your relationship with your Higher Power help you live more effectively?
6. What can you do to make this relationship better?

Actualize

1. What wisdom, as it relates to dealing with people, have you learned from these negative relationship experiences?
2. What have you learned about yourself as a result of these negative relationship experiences?

Utilize

1. What wisdom have you gained from these negative relationship experiences that can help you in future relationships?

Stabilize

1. What person(s) has the most positive influence over your life?
2. What can you do to spend more time with this person(s)?

3. What person(s) has the most negative influence over your life?
4. What can you do to spend less time with this person(s)?

Desensitize

1. What steps will you take in the next 48 hours to eliminate contact with negative people?
2. What steps will you take in the next 48 hours to minimize interactions with people in your life whom you cannot eliminate contact totally (e.g. family or classmates)?

Post Session Activity

1. Building Healthy Relationships Activity: Now we are going to work to build a specific strategy for building a healthy social network of positive people and positive relationships.

   First, on the top half of a sheet of paper write down the names of five positive people in your life. Next to their names, I want you to write a sentence describing what steps you will make to spend quality time with each of these people.

   Next, on the bottom half of this same sheet of paper I want you to write down the names of five negative people in your life. Next to these names I want you to write a sentence describing how you will eliminate contact with these people. For those people for whom you cannot eliminate contact totally (e.g. mother) I want you to write a one-sentence strategy on how you will minimize contact with this person.

Therapist Provides Session Summary

SESSION 13

MANAGING EMOTIONS & CONTROLLING IMPULSES

Prior Session Healthy Relationships Activity Checkpoint

THERAPIST: "In the first few sessions we talked about some of your life challenges and how they were affecting you mentally and emotionally. We also talked about increasing your self-esteem, accomplishing your life goals, and building healthy relationships."

Since the last time we met do you feel like your life in these areas has gotten better, worse, or stayed about the same?" (Note: No matter how the client answers this question the therapist can still use the same suggested sequence of questioning to address the same problems or a new set of problems.)

Verbalize

1. Since the last time we met have your problems gotten better, worse or about the same?
2. Why do you think your problems have gotten better, worse, or are staying the same?
3. Explain to me where you are as it relates to the life issues we have been discussing.

Intellectualize

1. What thoughts usually cause you to become sad and/or angry?
2. Why do you think these thoughts affect you in this way?
3. What people usually cause you to become sad and/or angry?
4. Why do you think these people affect you in this way?

5. What types of situations usually cause you to become sad or angry?
6. Why do you think these situations affect you in this way?

Emotionalize

1. Please remind me; what parts of these problems are the most frustrating?
2. What is the most hurtful part of this situation?
3. In the past week or so, how often have you become angry over this situation?
4. How do you deal with this anger?
5. In the past week or so, how often have you become sad over this situation?
6. How do you deal with this sadness?
7. Have your emotions surrounding these problems recently caused you to make a bad decision? If so, explain.
8. Give me two examples of when your emotions recently caused you to make a bad decision.
9. How did you feel after you made this decision?
10. Do you ever feel like you are in a cycle of feeling bad, making a bad decision, and then feeling even worse than you did before?

Spiritualize

1. What can you say to yourself to help you not become overwhelmed when you experience strong negative emotions?
2. In the grand scheme of life, who is the person you would let down the most if you do not overcome your issues and achieve success?
3. In what ways do you feel your Higher Power is helping you in this situation?
4. How often do you communicate with your Higher Power regarding this situation?
5. How can your Higher Power help you to view your situation in a more positive light?

Actualize

1. Think about a few times when you were extremely sad or angry but did *not* make a bad decision. Why do you think you were still able to do the right thing even though you were so upset?

Utilize

1. How can you use this strength and ability again in the future to make sure you do not make bad decisions when you are experiencing uncomfortable emotions?
2. What other strengths can you use to make good decisions despite experiencing uncomfortable emotions?

Stabilize

1. Think about some of the negative thoughts about life you sometimes have. What positive thoughts can you use to replace these negative thoughts?
2. Who should you totally avoid to keep from feeling sad or angry?
3. Who should you limit contact with to avoid feeling so sad or angry?
4. What types of situations do you need to avoid so that you do not become sad or angry?

Desensitize

1. What negative life consequences have you experienced as a result of making emotional decisions?
2. What can you do to remind yourself of these types of consequences when you feel like making a bad decision?
3. Who can you talk to when you feel like making a bad decision?

4. What are some more positive ways you can express your anger and/or sadness?

Post Session Activity

1. Emotion Management Exercise: For the rest of today's session, we will work to create a strategy for productively expressing your emotions. The purpose of this activity is for you to build a strategy for making sure your emotions do not create new problems in your life.

Emotion Management Activity

1. Work with the client to identify the negative emotion he experiences the most.

   The negative emotion I typically experience is <u>sadness.</u>

2. Work with the client to outline three ways in which he will constructively alleviate or express this negative emotion.

   Emotion Expression Strategy #1 <u>I will listen to my happy playlist.</u>

   Emotion Expression Strategy #2 <u>I will go to the gym and workout.</u>

   Emotion Expression Strategy #3 <u>I will go visit my grandmother.</u>

Therapist Provides Session Summary

SESSION 14

MANAGING STRESS, TIME, AND RESPONSIBILITIES

Prior Session Managing Emotions Activity Checkpoint

THERAPIST: "We have discussed your life challenges and how they are affecting you mentally and emotionally. We have also talked about increasing your self-esteem, accomplishing your life goals, and building healthy relationships. Last time we talked about how to effectively manage uncomfortable emotions. As I mentioned last time, these are very important aspects of life success. On the journey to success and positive growth things can become very stressful. Sometimes when we become stressed our weaknesses begin to show and we can begin to lose focus and motivation. Let's talk about stress and some of the things you can do to successfully manage your stress."

Verbalize

1. On a scale of 1 to 10, with 1 being "not stressed at all" and 10 being "overwhelmingly stressed", what is your current stress level?
2. What three things are stressing you out the most?
3. How long have you been experiencing these stressors?

Intellectualize

1. Which of these stressors are controllable (Self-Induced/Avoidable).
2. Which of these stressors are uncontrollable (Life-Induced/Unavoidable).
3. Stress usually comes as a result of a person feeling like they

lack the resources they need to handle life responsibilities. What do you feel you personally lack (e.g. time, money, support, etc.) in regards to being able to handle these situations?

4. What negative thoughts surround your stressor/situation?
5. How often do you have these thoughts?
6. What people play the biggest role in your current stress level?
7. What things do you do to add to your stress levels?
8. What bad decisions have you made in the past when you were stressed out?
9. What were the consequences of these bad decisions?

Emotionalize

1. How has your stress impacted you emotionally?
2. Is stress more likely to make you angry or sad?
3. Have you ever taken your anger or sadness out on yourself or others?

Spiritualize

1. Are there any stressors in your life that you should turn over to your Higher Power?
2. Why has it been hard for you to turn this stressor over to your Higher Power?
3. What can you do in the next few days to gradually turn this stressor over to your Higher Power?

Actualize

1. What are your two primary weaknesses?
2. Why do you consider these your primary weaknesses?
3. Are these weaknesses even worse when you are stressed out?
4. What are your two primary strengths?
5. Why do you consider these your primary strengths?

Utilize

1. When you are stressed out how can you use your strengths to overpower your weaknesses?
2. What can you do to make your strengths even stronger?
3. What can you do to manage your time better?

Stabilize

1. What role does poor time management play in your current stress levels?
2. What can you do to manage your time better? (Provide the client with a planner or a specific time management approach.)
3. Now I want you to make a to-do list of things you need to take care of over the course of the next two weeks.
4. Now I want you to imagine yourself accomplishing these goals and completing your list of to-dos. How do you feel as you imagine this success? Do you think you will feel this way when you accomplish these goals and complete your list of to-dos in real life?
5. What are your favorite hobbies? (Encourage the client to make time in his schedule to engage in their identified hobbies.)
6. Have you ever tried deep-breathing relaxation techniques? (Therapist should demonstrate deep-breathing relaxation techniques for client.)

Desensitize

1. Do you ever have trouble saying "no" to people? (Teach client to say "no" via role-play and/or rehearsal.)
2. Do you drink or use recreational substances? (Therapist should encourage client to develop a strategy to eliminate or minimize drug and alcohol use.)
3. Do you find time to enjoy life and laugh a little? (Therapist should work with client to identify ways to use humor as a form of stress management.)

4. What type of music makes you feel good about life and yourself? (Therapist should encourage client to create an empowering musical playlist.)

Post Session Activity

1. Stress Management Exercise: "Before we end today's session you will to develop a strategy for better managing your stress. If you effectively manage your stress you will live a more productive, healthy, and happier life."
2. Deep-Breathing Relaxation Technique: "For the next seven days I want you to use deep breathing exercises to manage your stress and anxiety. For the next seven days when you feel tense, stressed, or anxious, I want you to take deep slow breaths to naturally calm your mind and body. The way deep-breathing relaxation works is like this, first you breathe deeply and slowly through your nose. Once you have inhaled as deeply as you can, hold your breath for a few seconds and then exhale slowly until you have released as much air as you can."
3. Client should be provided with a small pocket-sized planner. Therapist and client should work to outline a list of all of the client's responsibilities (to-do list) for the next two weeks.
4. Therapist can instruct the client to create a 60-minute relaxing musical playlist that he can listen to during times when he is feeling stressed or anxious.

Therapist Provides Session Summary

SESSION 15

DEVELOPING A STIGMA DESENSITIZATION AND PRODUCTIVE DECISION-MAKING STRATEGY

Prior Session Managing Stress, Time and Responsibilities Activity Checkpoint

THERAPIST: "By now you know that as a Black male you will sometimes be treated differently because of the color of your skin. Because of this, it is important that you have a psychological defense system in place to protect youself from believing these negative messages and experiencing negative thoughts and emotions. If you do not have a psychological defense system in place you will believe those negative messages, internalize them, and start to behave in a way that will get in the way of your ability to have a happy and successful life. What we are going to do now is discuss specifically how you are going to begin to think, feel, and respond to future experiences of racism and negative messages."

"Basically, we are going to develop a strategy that you are going to use to cope, remain balanced, and productively adapt to living in a racist environment. This strategy will keep you from making bad decisions as a result of the emotional discomfort you sometimes feel as a Black male living in America. What we will be doing is identifying the people, places, things, and events that usually give you bad messages about you and your future. We will also be working to identify how these hurtful emotions sometimes cause you to make bad decisions and behave in ways that create problems for your life. When faced with racism and stigma, this psychological defense system will help you control your thoughts and channel your emotions in a way that makes your life better."

Verbalize

1. Client will verbalize any concerns he has about his ability to protect himself from stigma internalization and bad decision-making.

Intellectualize

1. Client articulates a thorough understanding of what he has learned about the negative thoughts and perceptions that are potentially a result of living in a stigmatizing environment.
2. Client articulates a thorough understanding of what he has learned as it relates to how these negative thoughts and perceptions potentially affect his decisions and behaviors.
3. Client articulates a thorough understanding of what types of stigmatizing messages are most tempting to believe/accept.
4. Client articulates a specific strategy for how he will increase his ability to protect himself from internalizing negative messages about who he is as a Black male.
5. Client articulates a specific strategy for how he will increase his ability to protect himself from internalizing negative messages about what his future holds as a result of being a Black male.

Emotionalize

1. Client articulates a thorough understanding of how negative messages about who he is as a Black male can cause negative emotions and feelings.
2. Client will articulate how negative emotions can produce an impulse to engage in destructive behavior patterns (maladaptive coping).

3. Client will articulate a thorough understanding of how destructive behavior patterns (maladaptive coping) can produce and sustain current and future problems.
4. Client articulates a specific strategy for how he will increase his ability to productively manage and express his emotions.
5. Client articulates the specific steps he will take to access his emotional support system when he is experiencing uncomfortable emotions.

Spiritualize

1. Client is able to clearly define a specific meaning and purpose for why it is important for him not to internalize the negative messages about Black males.
2. Client will outline a process for improving his relationship with his Higher Power.
3. Client will clearly state why it is important to his family, his faith, and the rest of the world that he ultimately accomplishes his life goals.

Actualize

1. Client will identify his primary strengths and abilities.
2. Client will identify his primary weaknesses and hang-ups.
3. Client will identify life lessons he has learned as a result of being a Black male in America.
4. Client will clearly identify how his race-related life challenges have made him a better person.

Utilize

1. Client will clearly identify how he will use his strengths to accomplish his life goals.
2. Client will clearly identify how he will use his strengths to overcome future race-related life challenges.

3. Client will clearly identify how he will use his strengths to help other people overcome their race-related life challenges.
4. Client will identify two people he will reach out to when he needs to discuss his race-related stress and challenges.

Stabilize

1. Client and therapist will review strategy from beginning to end.

Desensitize

1. The therapist will inform the client that if at any time he begins to feel overwhelmed with life, begins to engage in bad decision-making, or feels he is struggling not to internalize stigma, he is free to schedule a maintenance appointment.

Post Session Activity

1. Client will review the developed strategy at least one time per day for the next seven days. After the first seven days, the client will review the developed strategy one time per week until the next maintenance session.

Therapist Provides Session Summary

Note: Therapist will schedule bi-monthly maintenance sessions for one calendar year.

Stigma Internalization Therapy: A Strength Based Racially-Appropriate Intervention
CONCLUSION

We live in a race-sensitive, race-driven, and racially-divided society. In this intensely racialized climate, Black boys and Black men are disempowered by psychologically taxing forms of stigmatic social experiences. Against all odds, Black boys are still tasked with achieving the American Dream despite a "holistic lack" of available resources (i.e. racial capital, financial security, psychological sophistication, fraternal support, age-related social restrictions, etc.). This holistic lack of resources in the face of American racism and stigma complicates a Black boy's life journey. In the face of such a daunting task, many Black boys acquire an internal sense of hopelessness, which all too often negatively influences their motivation and engagement with the process of acquiring the American Dream.

The purpose of Stigma Internalization Therapy is to make the Black male invulnerable to his environmental risks. The SIT philosophy asserts that in order for Black males to experience sustained progress, they require engagement in developmental activities and experiences that possess racially-appropriate stimuli (i.e. people, info, ideas, activities, experiences, historical context, motivational cues, etc.) that inherently increase their "Spirit of Resilience". Such activities and experiences are necessary for effectively addressing the race-specific needs of Black males. Again, the purpose of SIT is resiliency building (i.e. making the Black male invulnerable to his environmental risks). In order for this invulnerable Black male to be created, he must develop a resistance to racial threats and acquire a profound attachment to a sense of confidence in his personal ability. Furthermore, he must acquire a deep-seated attachment to a sense of hope for his future.

The SIT model has the inherent ability (due to its racial and cultural relevance) to enhance a Black male's motivation, confidence, hope, and resilience. The SIT model utilizes a racially-appropriate questioning sequence designed to engage Black males in the level of critical thinking and life-analysis necessary for connecting to, and staying in touch with, the internal and external assets he has at his disposal. The SIT therapeutic approach also utilizes a package of psychologically engaging activities and exercises that function with the purpose of motivating, informing, instructing, and recalibrating the Black male client.

These internal and external assets minimize the potential negative impact of racism, stigma, and discrimination on the life journey of the Black male. SIT utilizes the internal resources (psychological) which a client comes into therapy already possessing. SIT also uses the external resources available to Black males at the onset of therapy as well as external resources identified during the course of therapy. Internal strengths include persistence, openness, spirituality, cultural pride, optimism, hope, readiness for change, etc.

External strengths include the people, places, and things that positively influence the client's life outside of therapy. These external client factors may include a supportive spouse, informative parents, church membership, mentorships, organizational participation, etcetera. When Black males are presented with environmental stimuli they can culturally translate, they are more likely to engage with the information and inspiration the environment is attempting to communicate.

The SIT approach is measured by its ability to help Black males withstand the pressures of racism, stigma, and discrimination. SIT is a defensive approach in that it assists Black males in the process of psychologically opposing toxic environmental challenges and resistant social forces. SIT recalibrates the Black male to the internal and external resources that can psychologically protect him from the challenges of life and reality. The SIT approach is also offensive (opposite of defensive) in that it enables a Black male to exert consistent levels of energy and counter-resistance onto opposing societal forces. The goal of SIT is to empower a Black male to exert a will and resilience stronger than his environmental challenges. This strength and will allows a Black male client to have personal power over his reality.

Counseling centers and educational systems have great transformational potential as it relates to impacting individuals and communities. These entities must clearly understand and embrace their moral responsibility to use research to write the rules and data to make the decisions. This respect for research has to be achieved in order to effectively confront the immediate need for racially-responsive models that address the psychosocial barriers to empowerment plaguing Black males in this country.

The ultimate question driving the national conversation on educating Black males is, what can be done to improve the social health of this portion of the population? Due to the maze of racism, stigma, and discrimination in American society, Black males require structured pathways that are racially-appropriate in order for them to find their way to the American Dream. The SIT model of therapy can serve as a portion of a community's pipeline forv protecting, nurturing, and guiding its young Black males to a life of fulfillment, prosperity, and happiness.

Concluding Remarks: US-Actualization = U.S.-Actualization

As our young nation continues its steady evolution, the collective soul of America is becoming increasingly diversified. The benefits of a culturally and racially-diversified nation are boundless as it relates to the exponential evolutionary leap that can only come through the merging of diversified intelligences, personalities, cultures, viewpoints, etc. The consequences that will emerge if these potential benefits are not realized include the nationwide production of anger, confusion, chaos, and conflict that can potentially incite exponential levels of evolutionary regression. In order for America to build the momentum necessary to break through the next stage of its' young development, there must be a deliberate effort on the part of mainstream America to utilize the social and cultural assets of the Black male. America must correct its philosophically deprived practice of inferiorizing the genius of the Black male.

If America can truly once and for all, pursue this agenda, America will empowr and fuel this Nation's evolutionary progress towards nation-actualization (i.e. the ability of a nation to reach its fullest potential). Through America's ability and willingness to utilize the unique potentials, relevant viewpoints, and valuable personalities of the Black male, America's goals of nation-actualization will be made more realistic and attainable. When America learns to sincerely value, respect, and celebrate the Black male through the inclusion of his relevant

traits, attributes, virtues, and perspectives, America will be on an accelerated path towards national progress and international leadership. Such international leadership can only be vested when America's diverse community can effectively, as one nation, focus its collective power, passion, and voice towards improving and accelerating the progress of all of its citizens. Then and only then will America be qualified to serve as a world leader directing other nations in our global community towards nation-actualization.

Investing in the Soul, Intelligence, and Gifts of the Black Male

America has been notorious for its insistence on excluding and/or belittling the social capital of Black males. Historically, the collective voice of the Black male has been silenced and/or ignored by White America's fear of sharing power with racial Minorities. This fear is founded on White America's fear of losing its place of power and position in the national and international community. This fear has led to the systematic practice of discrediting the priceless racial capital of the Black male. This fear is the fuel that drives the propaganda of Black male inferiority.

America is constrained by an ideology that refuses to acknowledge and include the moral, spiritual, psychological, and intellectual resources of the Black male. This inhibiting national perspective continues to stagnate, at numerous levels, our country's pursuit towards nation-actualization. The ability for the Black male gift to be a benefit to humankind is directly associated with the ability and opportunity for Black males to fully and truly have an opportunity to participate in the American Story.

In conclusion to this book, America's ultimate worth is precluded by its willingness and ability to value the history, struggles, victories, and visions of the Black male. When America makes a focused effort to respect and celebrate the unique cultural resources available to our society via the Black male, this Nation will place itself in a position to be the global leader of other societies who also are on their national journeys towards nation-actualization. This could lead to the initiation of unified forward progress of all nations, races, and cultures. This world progress via diversity and inclusion is the closest any of us will ever come to experiencing world peace! Due to its mixing pot nature, America has the greatest potential for teaching other nations how to humbly, yet passionately, produce a sense of community amongst the varying individuals that make up their societies. Once America successfully includes all categories of its citizens, America will be able to confidently serve as the measuring stick by which all societies, governments, and nations are evaluated as it relates to social morality and respect for humanity.

BIBLIOGRAPHY

Allen, L., & Mitchell, C. (1998). Racial and ethnic differences in patterns of problematic and adaptive development: An epidemiological review. In V. C. McLoyd & L. Steinberg (Eds.), *Studying minority adolescents: Conceptual, methodological, and theoretical issues* (pp. 29-54). Mahwah, NJ: Lawrence Erlbaum Associates.

Allport, G. W. (1954). *The nature of prejudice*. Cambridge, MA: Perseus Books.

Armistead, L., McCombs, A., Forehand, R., Wierson, M., Long, N., & Fauber, R. (1990). Coping with divorce: A study of young adolescents. *Journal of Clinical Child Psychology, 19,* 79-84.

Armstead, C. A., Lawler, K. A., Gorden, G., Cross, J., & Gibbons, J. (1989). Relationship of racial stressors to blood pressure responses and anger expression in Black college students. *Health Psychology*, *8,* 541-556.

Asante, M. K. (1990). *Kemet, Afrocentricity and knowledge.* Trenton, NJ: Africa World Press, Inc.

Ayers, T. S. (1991). *A dispositional and situational assessment of children's coping: Testing alternative theoretical models* (Unpublished doctoral dissertation). Arizona State University, Tempe.

Ayers, T. S., Sandler, I. N., West, S. G., & Roosa, M. W. (1996). A dispositional and situational assessment of children's coping. *Journal of Personality, 64,* 923-958.

Barbarin, O., & Soler, R. (1993). Behavioral, emotional and academic adjustment in a national probability sample of African American children: Effects of age, gender and family structure. *Journal of Black Psychology, 19,* 423-446.

Barrios, B. A., & Hartmann, D. P. (1997). Fears and anxieties. In E. J. Mash & L. G. Terdal (Eds.), *Assessment of childhood disorders* (3rd ed., pp. 230-327). New York: Guilford Press.

Beck, A., Brown, G., Steer, R., Eidelson, J., & Riskind, J. (1987). Differentiating anxiety and depression: A test of the cognitive content-specificity hypothesis. *Journal of Abnormal Psychology, 96,* 179-183.

Beck, A. T., Steer, R. A., & Brown, G. K. (1996). *Beck Depression Inventory–Second Edition (BDI-II): Manual:* San Antonio, TX: Pearson.

Berlin, I. (2010). *The making of African America: The four great migrations.* New York: Viking.

Biafora, F. A., Taylor, D. L.,Warheit, G. J., Zimmerman, R. S., & Vega, W. A. (1993). Cultural mistrust and racial awareness among ethnically diverse Black adolescent boys. *Journal of Black Psychology, 19*, 266-281.Blank, W. (1997). Authentic instruction. In W. E. Blank & S. Harwell (Eds.), *Promising practices for connecting high school to the real world* (pp. 15-21). Tampa, FL: University of South Florida.

Bok, D., & Bowen, W. G. (1998). *The shape of the river: Long-term consequences of considering race in college and university admissions.* Princeton, NJ: Princeton University Press.

Bovbjerg, D. H., Guevarra, J. S., Kwate, N. O., & Valdimarsdottir, H. B. (2003). Experiences of racist events are associated with negative health consequences for African American women. *Journal of the National Medical Association, 95,* 450-460.

Boyd, A. & Franklin, N. (2000). Invisibility syndrome: A clinical model of the effects of racism on African-American males. *American Journal of Orthopsychiatry. 70,* 33-41.

Boykin, W. (1986). The triple quandary in the schooling of Afro-American children. In U. Neisser (Ed.), *The school achievement of minority children* (pp. 57-92). Hillsdale, NJ: Lawrence Erlbaum.

Branscombe, N. R., Schmitt, M. T., & Harvey, R. D. (1999). Perceiving pervasive discrimination among African Americans: Implications for group identification and well-being. *Journal of Personality and Social Psychology, 77,* 135-149.

Broman, C. L. (1997). Race-related factors and life satisfaction among African Americans. *Journal of Black Psychology, 23,* 36-49.

Broman, C. L. (2000). Drug use among African-Americans. *Encyclopedia of Criminology and Deviant Behavior*. Philadelphia: Brunner-Routledge.

Brondolo, E., Rieppi R., Erickson, S. A., Bagiella, E., Shapiro, P. A. & McKinley, P. (2003). Hostility, interpersonal interactions, and ambulatory blood pressure. *Psychosomatic Medicine, 65,* 1003-1011.

Brown, T. N., Williams, D. R., Jackson, J. S., Sellers, S. L., Brown, K. T., & Torres, M. (2000). 'Being Black and feeling blue': The mental health consequences of racial discrimination. *Race and Society, 2,* 117-131.

Burke, A. W. (1984). Racism and psychological disturbance among West Indians in Britain. *The International Journal of Social Psychiatry, 30,* 50-68.

Calabrese, R. L., & Poe, J. (1990). Alienation: An explanation of high dropout rates among African American and Latino students. *Educational Research Quarterly, 14,* 22-26.

Caldwell, C., Kohn-Wood, L. P., Schmeelk-Cone, K. H., Chavous, T.M., & Zimmerman, M. A. (2004). Racial discrimination and racial identity as risk or protective factors for violent behaviors in African American young adults. *American Journal of Community Psychology, 33*, 91-105.

Cantwell, D. (1990). Depression across the early life span, In M. Lewis & M. Miller (Eds.), *Handbook of developmental psychopathology* (pp. 293-309). New York: Plenum Press.

Carter, R. T., & Goodwin, A. L. (1994). Racial identity and education. *Review of Research in Education, 20,* 291-336.

Cartwright, D. (1950). Emotional dimensions of group life. In M. L. Raymert (Ed.), *Feelings and emotions* (pp. 439-477). New York: McGraw-Hill Press.

Cauce, A. M., Ryan, K. D., & Grove, K. (1998). Children and adolescents of color, where are you? Participation, selection, recruitment, and retention in developmental research. In V. C. McLoyd & L. Steinberg (Eds.), *Studying conceptual, methodological, and theoretical issues* (pp. 147-166). Mahwah, NJ: Lawrence Erlbaum Associates.

Centers for Disease Control and Prevention. (2006). *The health consequences of involuntary exposure to tobacco smoke: A report of the Surgeon General.* Atlanta, GA: U.S. Department of Health and Human Services. Retrieved from http://www.cdc.gov/tobacco/data_statistics/sgr/sgr_2006/index.htm

Chandra, A., & Batada, A. (2006). Exploring stress and coping among urban African-American adolescents: The shifting the lens study. *Preventing Chronic Disease, 3,* 1-10.

Chang, E. C. (1998). Dispositional optimism and primary and secondary appraisal of a stressor: Controlling for confounding influences and relations to coping and psychological and physical adjustment. *Journal of Personality and Social Psychology, 74,* 1109-1120.

Clark, R. (2003). Parental history of hypertension and coping responses predict blood pressure changes to a perceived racism speaking task in black college volunteers. *Psychosomatic Medicine, 65*(6), 1012-1019.

Clark, R., Anderson, N. B., Clark, V. R., & Williams, D. R. (1999). Racism as a stressor for African Americans: A biopsychosocial model. *American Psychologist, 54,* 805-816.

Clark, R., Novak, J. D., & Dupree, D. (2002). Relationship of perceived parenting practices to anger regulation and coping strategies in African-American adolescents. *Journal of Adolescence, 25,* 373-384.

Cohen, S., Karmarck, T., & Mermelstein, R. (1983). A global measure of perceived stress. *Journal of Health and Social Behavior, 24,* 385-396.

Coll, C., Lamberty, G., Jenkins, R., McAdoo, H. P., Crnic, K., Wasik, B. H., Garcia, H. V. (1996). An integrative model for the study of developmental competencies in minority children. *Child Development, 67,* 1891-1914.

Comer, J. P. (1995). Racism and African American adolescent development. In C. V. Willie, P. P. Rieker, B. M. Kramer, & B. S. Brown (Eds.), *Mental health, racism, and sexism* (pp. 151-170). Pittsburgh, PA: University of Pittsburgh Press.

Compas, B. E., Connor-Smith, J. K., Saltzman, H., Thomsen, A. H., & Wadsworth, M. E. (2001). Coping with stress during childhood and adolescence: Problems, progress, and potential in theory and research. *Psychological Bulletin, 127,* 87-112.

Compas, B. E., Malcarne, V. L., & Fondacaro, K. M. (1988). Coping with stressful events in older children and young adolescents. *Journal of Counseling and Clinical Psychology, 56*, 405-411.

Compas, B. E., Orosan, P. G., & Grant, K. E. (1993). Adolescent stress and coping: Implications for psychopathology during adolescence. *Journal of Adolescence, 16,* 331-349.

Conrad, C. A., & Lowery, M. (1995). Race, earnings, and intelligence. *Black Enterprise, 25,* 26-31.

Contrada, R. J., Ashmore, R. D., Gary, M. L. Coups, E. Egeth, J. D. Sewell, A., Ewell, K., Goyal, T., & Chasse, V. (1999). *Measure of ethnicity related stress: Psychometric properties, ethnic group differences and association with well-being.* Unpublished manuscript, Rutgers University.

Cosway, R., Endler, N. S., Sadler, A. J., & Deary, I. J. (2000). The Coping Inventory for Stressful Situations: Factorial structure and associations with personality traits and psychological health. *Journal of Applied Biobehavioral Research, 5,* 121-143.

Danoff-Burg, S., Perlow, H. M., & Swenson, R. R. (2004). Hope and life satisfaction in Black college students coping with race-related stress. *Journal of Black Psychology, 30*(2), 208-228.

Department of Education and Employment. (2001). *Schools: Building on success.* London: DfEE.

Diaz, R., Ayala, G., & Bien, E. (2004). Sexual risks as an outcome of social oppression: Data from a probability sample of Latino gay men in three US cities. *Cultural Diversity and Ethnic Minority Psychology, 10,* 255-267.

Duckitt, J. (1992). Psychology and prejudice: A historical analysis and framework. *American Psychologist, 47,* 1182-1193.

Durant, R.H., Cadenhead, C., Pendergrast, R. A., Slavens, G., & Linder, C. W. (1994). Factors associated with the use of violence among urban black adolescents. *American Journal of Public Health, 84,* 612-617.

Dutton, G., Ancon, M., Jones, G., & Brantley, P. (2005). Validation of the Beck Depression Inventory–II in a low income African American sample of medical outpatients. *Psychological Assessment, 17,* 110-114.

Ebata, A. T., & Moss, R. H. (1991). Coping and adjustment in healthy and distressed adolescents. *Journal of Applied Development Psychology, 12,* 33-54.

Eckholm, E. (2006, March 20). Plight thickens for Black men, study warns. *New York Times.* Retrieved from http://www.nytimes.com/2006/03/20/national/20blackmen.html?pagewanted=all&_r=0

Eldermen, P., Holzer, H. J., & Offner, P. (2006). *Reconnecting disadvantaged young men.* Washington, DC: Urban Institute Press.

Endler, N. S., & Parker, J. D. A. (1988). *The Assessment of Coping: The multidimensional coping inventory*. Department of Psychology Reports, York University, Toronto, ON,

No.174.

Endler, N. S., & Parker, J. D. A. (1990a). *Coping Inventory for Stressful Situations (CISS): Manual.* Toronto, ON: Multi-Health Systems.

Endler, N. S., & Parker, J. D. A. (1990b). The multidimensional assessment of coping: A critical evaluation. *Journal of Personality and Social Psychology, 58,* 844-854.

Endler, N. S., & Parker, J. D. A. (1999). *Coping Inventory for Stressful Situations (CISS): Manual* (2nd ed.). North Tonawanda, NY: Multi-Health Systems.

Entwistle, N. J. (1968). Academic motivation and school attainment. *British Journal of Educational Psychology, 38,* 181-188.

Erikson, E. (1956). The problems of ego identity. *Journal of American Psychoanalytic Association, 4*, 56-121.

Essed, P. (1990). *Everyday racism: Reports from women of two cultures.* Claremont, CA: Hunter House.

Essed, P. (1991). *Understanding everyday racism: An interdisciplinary theory.* London: Sage.

Feagin, J. R., & Barnett, B. M. (2005). Success and failure: How systemic racism trumped the *Brown v. Board of Education* decision. *University of Illinois Law Review, 2004*(5).

Fein, S., & Spencer, S. J. (1997). Prejudice as self-image maintenance: Affirming the self through derogating others. *Journal of Personality and Social Psychology, 73,* 31-44.

Feldman, S. S., & Elliot, G. R. (1990). *At the threshold: The developing adolescent.* Cambridge, MA: Cambridge University Press.

Felice, L. (1981). Black student drop-out behavior: Disengagement from school, rejection, and racial discrimination. *Journal of Negro Education, 50,* 415-424.

Fine, M. (1991). *Framing dropouts: Notes on the politics of an urban school.* Albany: State University of New York Press.

Fischer, A. R., & Shaw, C. M. (1999). African Americans' mental health and perceptions of racist discrimination: The moderating effects of racial socialization experiences and self-esteem. *Journal of Counseling Psychology, 46,* 395-407.

Folkman, S., & Lazarus, R. (1984). *Stress appraisal, and coping.* New York: Springer.

Ford, D. Y. (1992). The American achievement ideology as perceived by urban African American students – Exploration by gender and academic program. *Urban Education, 27*, 196-211.

Fordham, S., & Ogbu, J. (1986). Black students' school success: Coping with the burden of acting white. *Urban Review, 18,* 176-206.

Fray, J. C. (1993). Hypertension in Blacks: Physiological, psychosocial, theoretical and therapeutic challenges. In J. C. S. Fray, & J. G. Douglas (Eds.), *Pathophysiology of hypertension in blacks* (pp. 3-22). New York: Oxford University Press.

Freedle, R. O. (2003). Correcting the SAT's ethnic and social-class bias: A method for reestimating SAT Scores. *Harvard Educational Review, 73,* 1-38.

Fuentes, A. (2003). DISCIPLINE AND PUNISH: Zero tolerance policies have created a "lockdown" environment in schools. *The NATION, 277*(20), 17-19.

Garibaldi, A. M. (1997). Four decades of progress . . . and decline: An assessment of African American education attainment. *The Journal of Negro Education, 2,* 105-120.

Gaylord, H., Noni, K., Gipson, P., Mance, G., & Grant, K. E. (2008). Coping patterns of African American adolescents: A confirmatory factor analysis and cluster analysis of the Children's Coping Behaviors Checklist. *Psychological*

Assessment, 20(1), 10-22.

Germain, C. B., & Gitterman, A. (1987). Ecological perspective. In A. Minahan (Ed.), *Encyclopedia of Social Work* (18th ed., Vol. 1, pp. 488-499). Silver Spring, MD: National Association of Social Workers.

Gibbons, F., Gerrard, M., & Cleveland, M. (2004). Perceived discrimination and substance use in African American parents and their children: A panel study. *Journal of Personality and Social Psychology, 86,* 517-529.

Goffman, E. (1963). *Stigma: Notes on the management of a spoiled identity*. New York: Simon and Schuster.

Gold, S. J. (2004). From Jim Crow to racial hegemony: Evolving explanations of racial hierarchy. *Ethnic and Racial Studies, 27,* 951-968.

Gougis, R. A. (1986). The effects of prejudice and stress on the academic performance of Black-Americans. In U. Neisser (Ed.), *The school achievement of minority children: New perspective* (pp. 145-158). Hillsdale, NJ: Lawrence Erlbaum Associates.

Graham, M., & Robinson, G. (2004). The silent catastrophe: Institutional racism in the British educational system and the underachievement of black boys. *Journal of Black Studies, 34,* 653-681.

Graham, S. (1989). Motivation in Afro Americans. In G. L. Berry & J. K. Asamen (Eds.), *Black students: Psychological issues and academic achievement* (pp. 40-68). Newbury Park, CA: Sage.

Graham S. (1991). A review of attribution theory in achievement contexts. *Educational Psychological Review, 3,* 5-39.

Graham, S. (1994). Motivation in African Americans. *Review of Educational Research, 64,* 55-118.

Grant, C. A., & Sleeter, C. (1988). Race, class, and gender and abandoned dreams. *Teachers College Record, 90,* 19-40.

Grant, K. E., O'Koon, J. H., Davis, T. H., Roache, N. A., Poindexter, L. M., & Armstrong, M. L. (2000). Protective factors affecting low-income urban African American youth exposed to stress. *Journal of Early Adolescence, 20,* 388-417.

Hagan, J., & Peterson, R. (1995). Criminal inequality in America. In J. Hagan and R. Peterson (Eds.), *Crime and inequality* (pp. 14-36). Stanford, CA: Stanford University Press.

Harrell, S. (1995). *The Racism and Life Experience Scale–Brief Version.* Unpublished manuscript.

Harrell, S. P. (2000). A multidimensional conceptualization of racism-related stress: Implications for the well-being of people of color. *American Journal of Orthopsychiatry, 70,* 42-57.

Harris, J. J., & Ford, D. Y. (1991). Identifying and nurturing the promise of gifted Black American children. *Journal of Negro Education, 60,* 3-18.

Harter, S., & Connell, J. P. (1984). A model of the relationship among children's academic achievement and their self-perceptions of competence, control, and motivational orientation. In J. Nichols (Ed.), *The development of achievement motivation* (pp. 219–250). Greenwich, CT: JAI Press.

Haycock, K. (2001). Closing the achievement gap. *Educational Leadership, 58*(6), 6-11.

Helms, J. E. (2002). A remedy for the Black–White test-score disparity. *American Psychologist, 57,* 303–305.

Herman, K. C., Ostrander, R., & Tucker, C. M. (2007). Do family environments and negative cognitions of adolescents with depressive symptoms vary by ethnic group? *Journal of Family Psychology, 21*, 325-330.

Herman-Stahl, M. A., Stemmler, M., & Petersen, A. C. (1995).

Approach and avoidant coping: Implications for adolescent mental health. *Journal of Youth and Adolescence, 24,* 649-665.

Hobfoll, S. (2001). The influence of culture, community, and the nest-self in the stress process: Advancing conservation of resources theory. *Applied Psychology: An International Review, 50*, 337-421.

Irvine, J. (1990). *Black students and school failure: Policies, practices, and prescriptions.* New York: Praeger.

Irvine, J. J. (1991). *Culturally responsive and responsible pedagogy: The inclusion of culture, research, and reflection in the knowledge base of teacher education.* Paper presented at the annual meeting of the American Association of Colleges for Teacher Education, Atlanta, GA.

Jackson, J. S., Brown, T. N., Williams, D. R., Torres, M., Sellers, S .L., & Brown, K. (1996). Racism and the physical and mental health status of African Americans: A thirteen year national panel study. *Ethnicity and Disease, 6,* 132-147.

Jackson, J. S., Williams, D. R., & Torres, M. (1997). In A. Maney (Ed.), *Perceptions of discrimination: The stress process and physical and psychological health.* Washington, DC: National Institute for Mental Health.

Jacoby, R., & Glauberman, N. (1995). *The bell curve debate.* New York: Random House.

Jaynes, G. D., & Williams, R. M. (1989). *A common destiny: Blacks and American society.* Washington DC: National Research Council/National Academy Press.

Jones, J. M. (1972). *Prejudice and racism.* Reading, MA: Addison-Wesley.

Jones, J. M. (1997). *Prejudice and racism* (2nd ed.). New York: McGraw Hill.

Jones, R. (1999). *Teaching racism or tackling it? Multicultural stories from White beginning teachers*. London: Trentham.

Jost, J. T., & Hunyady, O. (2002). The psychology of system justification and the palliative function of ideology. *European Review of Social Psychology, 13,* 111–153.

Kaufmann, Y. (1989). Analytical psychotherapy. In R. J. Corsini & D. Wedding (Eds.), *Current psychotherapies* (4th ed., pp. 118-125). Itasca, IL: F. E. Peacock.

Kistner, J. A., David, C. F., & White, B. A. (2003). Ethnic and sex differences in children's depressive symptoms: Mediating effects of perceived and actual competence. *Journal of Clinical Child and Adolescent Psychology, 32*, 341-350.

Kistner, J. A., David-Ferdon, C. F., Lopez, C. M., & Dunkel, S.. (2007). Ethnic and sex differences in children's depressive symptoms. *Journal of Clinical Child and Adolescent Psychology, 36,* 171-181.

Klarmann, M. J. (2004). *From Jim Crow to civil rights: The Supreme Court and the struggle for racial equality.* New York: Oxford University Press.

Klonoff, E. A., Landrine, H., & Ullman, J. B. (1999). Racial discrimination and psychiatric symptoms among Blacks. *Cultural Diversity & Ethnic Minority Psychology, 5,* 329–339.

Kraaij, V., Garnefski, N., de Wilde, E. J., Dijkstra, A., Gebhardt, W., Maes, S., & Doest, L. (2003). Negative life events and depressive symptoms in late adolescence: Bonding and cognitive coping as vulnerability factors. *Journal of Youth and Adolescence, 32*, 185-193.

Krieger, N., & Sidney, S. (1996). Racial discrimination and blood pressure: The CARDIA study of young Black and White adults. *American Journal of Public Health, 86*, 1370-1378.

Kumar, G., Steer, R. A., Teitelman, K. B., & Villacis, L. (2002). Effectiveness of the Beck Depression Inventory-II subscales in screening for major depressive disorders in adolescent psychiatric inpatients. *Assessment, 9*, 164-170.

Kunjufu, J. (1984). *Developing positive self-images and discipline in black children.* Chicago, IL: African-American Images.

Landrine, H., & Klonoff, E. A. (1994). Cultural diversity in causal attributions for illness. *Journal of Behavioral Medicine, 17,* 181-193.

Landrine, H., & Klonoff, E. A. (1996). The schedule of racist events: A measure of racial discrimination and a study of its negative physical and mental consequences. *Journal of Black Psychology, 22*, 144-168.

Langley, K., Marshall, L., van den Bree, M., Thomas, H., Owen, M., O'Donovan, M., & Thapar, A. (2004). Association of the dopamine D4 receptor gene 7-repeat allele with neuropsychological test performance of children with ADHD. *American Journal of Psychiatry, 161*, 133-138.

Lee, R. M. (2003). Do ethnic identity and other-group orientation protect against discrimination for Asian Americans? *Journal of Counseling Psychology, 50*, 133-141.

Lee, S., Piersel, W., Frielander, R., & Collamer, W. (1988). Concurrent validity of the Revised Children's Manifest Anxiety scale (RCMAS) for adolescents. *Educational and Psychological Measurement, 48*, 429-433.

Levin, S., Federico, C., Sidanius, J., & Rabinowitz, J. (2002). Social dominance orientation and intergroup bias: The legitimation of favoritism for high-status groups. *Personality and Social Psychology Bulletin, 28*, 144-157.

Lester, J. (1968). *To be a slave.* New York: Dell.

Link, B. G., Struening, E. L., Rahav, M., Phelan, J., & Nuttbrock, L. (1997). On stigma and its consequences: Evidence from a longitudinal study of men with dual diagnoses of mental illness and substance abuse. *Journal of Health and Social Behavior, 38*, 177-190.

Major, B., Gramzow, R., McCoy, S. K., Levin, S., Schmader, T., & Sidanius, J. (2002). Perceiving personal discrimination: The role of group status and status legitimizing ideology. *Journal of Personality and Social Psychology, 80*, 782-796.

Major, B., Quinton, W. J., & McCoy, S. K. (2002). Antecedents and consequences of attributions to discrimination: Theoretical and empirical advances. In M. P. Zanna (Ed.), *Advances in experimental social psychology* (Vol. 34, pp. 251-330). New York: Academic Press.

Masters, J. C., Barden, C., & Ford, M. E. (1979). Affective state, expressive behavior and learning in children. *Journal of Personality and Social Psychology, 37*, 380-390.

Mauer, M. (1999). *Race to incarcerate.* New York: New Press.

McCord, C., & Freeman, H. P. (1990). Excess mortality in Harlem. *New England Journal of Medicine, 322*, 173-177.

McIlroy, D., & Bunting, D. (2002). Personality, behavior and academic achievement: Principles for educators to inculcate and students to model. *Contemporary Education Psychology, 27*, 326-337.

McWilliams, L. A., Cox, B. J., & Enns, M. W. (2003). Use of the Coping Inventory for Stressful Situations in a clinically depressed sample: Factor structure, personality correlates, and prediction of distress. *Journal of Clinical Psychology, 59*, 423–437.

Merikangas, K. R., & Angst, J. (1995). *The challenge of depressive disorders in adolescence.* Cambridge, UK: Cambridge University Press.

Merril, K. (2003). *Behavioral, social, and emotional assessment of children and adolescents* (2nd ed). Mahwah, NJ: Lawrence Erlbaum.

Moilanen, D. (1995). Validity of Beck's cognitive theory of depression with nonreferred adolescents. *Journal of*

Counseling and Development, 73, 438-442.

Moore, E. G. (1987). Ethnic social milieu and Black children's intelligence tests achievement. *Journal of Negro Education, 56*(1) 44-52.

Morris, R., & Kratochwill, T. (1983). *Treating children's fears and phobias*. New York: Pergamon.

National Center for Education Statistics. (2008). Retrieved October, 23, 2008 from http://nces.ed.gov 2008

Nazroo, J. Y. (2003). The structuring of ethnic inequalities in health: economic position, racial discrimination and racism. *American Journal of Public Health, 93*, 277-284.

Neville, H., Heppner, P., Ji, P., & Thye, R. (2004). The relations among general and race-related stressors and psychoeducational adjustment in Black students attending predominantly White institutions. *Journal of Black Studies, 34*, 599-618.

Newton, M., & Newton, J. A. (1991). *Racial and religious violence in America: A chronology*. New York, NY: Garland.

Nieto, S. (1991). *Affirming diversity: The sociopolitical context of multicultural education*. New York: Longman Press.

Nyborg, V. M., & Curry, J. F. (2003). The impact of perceived racism: Psychological symptoms among African American boys. *Journal of Clinical Child and Adolescent Psychology, 32*, 258-266.

Ogbu, J. (1986). The consequences of the American caste system. In U. Neisser (Ed.), *The school achievement of minority children: New perspectives* (pp. 19-56). Hillsdale, NJ: Lawrence Erlbaum Associates.

Ogbu, J. (1999). Beyond language: Ebonics proper English in Black America speech community. *American Education Research Journal, 36*, 147-184.

Ogbu, J. (2003). Black American students in an affluent suburb:

A study of academic disengagement. A volume in the Sociocultural, Political, and Historical Studies in Education Series. Mahwah: NJ: Erlbaum.

Ogbu, J. U. (1991). Low school performance as an adaption: The CASE of BLACKS in STOCKTON, CALIFORNIA. In M. GIBSON & J. OGBU (EDS.), MINORITY STATUS and SCHOOLING: A COMPARATIVE STUDY of IMMIGRANT and INVOLUNTARY MINORITIES (PP. 249-286). New York: Garland.

Ogbu, J. U. (1993). Variability in minority school performance: A problem in search of an explanation. In E. Jacob & C. Jordan (Eds.), *Minority education: Anthropological perspectives* (pp. 83-112). Norwood, NJ: Ablex.

Ogbu, J. U. (1994). Racial stratification and education in the U.S.: Why inequality persists. *Teachers College Record, 96*(2), 264-298.

Orfield, G. (2006). *Reviving the goal of an integrated society: A 21st century challenge.* Los Angeles, CA: The Civil Rights Project/Proyecto Derechos Civiles at UCLA.

Osman, A., Kopper, B. A., Barrios, F. X., Gutierrez, P. M., & Bagge, C. L. (2004). Reliability and validity of the Beck Depression Inventory-II with adolescent psychiatric inpatients, *Psychological Assessment, 16*, 120–132.

Outlaw, F. H. (1993). Stress and coping: The influence of racism on the cognitive appraisal processing of African Americans. *Issues in Mental Health Nursing, 14*, 399-409.

Pager, D., & Shepherd, H. (2008).The sociology of discrimination: Racial discrimination in employment, housing, credit, and consumer markets. *Annual Review of Sociology, 34*, 181-209.

Paikoff, R. L., & Brooks-Gunn, J. (1991). Do parent-child relationships change during puberty? *Psychological Bulletin, 110*, 47-66.

Petersen, A. C. (1988). *Adolescent development.* Palo Alto, CA: Annual Reviews.

Ponterotto, J. G., & Pedersen, P. B. (1993). *Preventing prejudice.* Newberry Park, CA: Sage.

Potts, R., Morse, M., Felleman, E., & Masters, J. C. (1986). Children's emotions and memory for affective narrative content. *Motivation and Emotion, 10*, 39-57.

Potts, R. G. (1997). The social construction and social marketing of the "dangerous African American man." *Journal of African American Men, 2*, 11-24.

Raffaele-Mendez, L. M., & Knoff, H. M. (2003). Who gets suspended from school and why: A demographic analysis of schools and disciplinary infractions in a large school district. *Education & Treatment of Children, 26*, 30-51.

Raffaele-Mendez, L. M., Knoff, H. M., & Ferron, J. M. (2002). School demographic variables and out-of-school suspension rates: A quantitative and qualitative analysis of a large, ethnically diverse school district. *Psychology in the Schools, 39*, 259-277.

Research Center on Academic Success (CRIRES). (2005). Retrieved from International Observatory on Academic Achievement: http://www.criresoirs.ulaval.ca/sgc/lang/en_CA/pid/5493

Reynolds, C. (1982). Convergent and divergent validity of the Revised Children's Manifest Anxiety Scale. *Educational and Psychological Measurement, 42*, 1205-1212.

Reynolds, C. R. (1980). Concurrent validity of what I think and feel: The Revised Children's Manifest Anxiety Scale. *Journal of Consulting and Clinical Psychology, 48*, 774-775.

Reynolds, C. R., & Richmond, B. O. (1978). What I think and feel: A revised measure of children's manifest anxiety. *Journal of Abnormal Child Psychology, 6*, 271-280.

Reynolds, C. R., & Richmond, B. O. (2008). *The Revised Children's Manifest Anxiety Scale: Manual.* Los Angeles, CA: Western Psychological Services.

Rinderman, H., & Neubauer, A. (2001). The influence of personality on three aspects of cognitive performance: Processing speed, intelligence and school performance. *Personality and Individual Differences, 30*, 829-842.

Roscigno, V. J. (2000). Family/school inequality and African-American/Hispanic achievement. *Social Problems, 47*, 266-290.

Rosenfeld, S. (1997). Labeling mental illness: The effects of received services and perceived stigma on life satisfaction. *American Sociological Review, 62*, 660-672.

Roth, S., & Cohen, L. J. (1986). Approach, avoidance, and coping with stress. *American Psychologist, 41*, 813-819.

Ruggiero, K. M., Taylor, D. M., & Lydon, J. (1997). How disadvantaged group members cope with discrimination when social support is available. *Journal of Applied Social Psychology, 27*, 1581-1600.

Russo, C. J., & Talbert-Johnson, C. (1997). The overrepresentation of African American children in special education: The resegregation of educational programming? *Education and Urban Society, 29*, 136-148.

Sable, J. (1998). *The educational progress of Black students.* Washington, DC: U.S. Government Printing Office.

Sabnani, H. B., & Ponterotto, J. G. (1992). Racial/ethnic minority-specific instrumentation in counseling research: A review, critique, and recommendations. *Measurement and Evaluation in Counseling and Development, 24*, 161-187.

Salts, C. J., Lindholm, B. W., & Goddard, H. W. (1995). Predictive variables of violent behavior in adolescent males. *Youth and Society, 26*, 377-399.

Sanders, M. G. (1997). Overcoming obstacles: Academic achievement as a response to racism and discrimination. *Journal of Negro Education, 66*, 83–93.

Sanders-Phillips K. (1999). Ethnic minority women, health behaviors, and drug abuse: A continuum of psychosocial risks. In M. D. Glantz & C. R. Hartel (Eds.), *Drug abuse: Origins and interventions* (pp. 191-217). Washington, DC: American Psychological Association.

Santogrossi, D., Durand, V., & Barlow, D. (2004). Abnormal psychology: An integrative approach (4th ed.). Belmont, CA: Wadsworth.

Sautner, B. (2001). Rethinking the effectiveness of suspensions. *Reclaiming Children and Youth, 9*, 210-214.

Scheier, M. F., & Carver, C. S. (1985). Optimism, coping, and health: Assessment and implications of generalized outcome expectancies. *Health Psychology, 4,* 219-247.

Scott, L. D. (2003). The relation of racial identity and racial socialization to coping with discrimination among African American adolescents. *Journal of Black Psychology, 33*, 520 –538.

Seaton, E. K. (2003). An examination of the factor structure of the Index of Race-Related Stress among a sample of African American adolescents, *Journal of Black Psychology, 29*, 292-307.

Seaton, E. K. (2006). Examination of a measure of racial discrimination among African American adolescents. *Journal of Applied Social Psychology, 36*, 1414-1429.

Seiffge-Krenke, I. (1995). *Stress, coping, and relationships in adolescence*. Mahwah, NJ: Erlbaum.

Simons, R. L., Murry, V., McLoyd, V., Lin, K., Cutrona, C., & Conger, R. D. (2002). Discrimination, crime, ethnic identity and parenting as correlates of depressive symptoms among African American children: a multilevel analysis.

Development and Psychopathology, 14, 371-393.

Simpson, G. E., & Yinger J. M. (1985). Racial and cultural minorities: An analysis of prejudice and discrimination (5th ed.). New York: Plenum.

Stark, C., Belbin, A., Hopkins, P., Gibbs, D., Hay, A., & Gunnell, D. (2006). Male suicide and occupation in Scotland. *Health Statistics Quarterly, 29,* 26-29.

Staveteig, S., & Wigton, A. (2000). *Racial and ethnic disparities: Key findings from the National Survey of America's Families.* Series B, No. B-5. Washington, DC: Urban Institute.

Steele, C. M. (1992, April). Race and the schooling of Black Americans. *The Atlantic Monthly, 269,* 68-78.

Steele, C. M. (1997). A threat in the air: How stereotypes shape intellectual identity and performance. *American Psychologist, 52,* 613–629.

Stevenson, H. C., Reed, J., Bodison, P., & Bishop, A. (1997). Racism stress management: Racial socialization beliefs and the experience of depression and anger in African American youth. *Youth & Society, 29,* 197-222.

Stryker, S., & Burke, P. J. (2000). *The past, present, and future of identity theory.* Newbury Park, CA: Sage.

Suarez-Balcazar, Y., Orellan-Damacela, L., Portillo, N., Rowan, J. M., & C. Andrews-Guillen. (2003). Experiences of differential treatment among college students of color. *The Journal of Higher Education, 74*, 428-444.

Tannenbaum, A. (1968). Values, attitudes, and behaviors in social science and society. *JOURNAL OF SOCIAL ISSUES, 24*(1).

Tatum, A. W. (2000). Breaking down barriers that disenfranchise African American adolescent readers in low-level tracks. *Journal of Adolescent & Adult Literacy, 44*(1), 52-64.

Tatum, A.W. (2002). Professional development for teachers

of African American adolescents. *Illinois Reading Council Journal, 30*(1), 42-52.

Tatum, B. (1996). The colonial model as a theoretical explanation of crime and delinquency. In A. Sulton (Ed.), *AFRICAN-AMERICAN perspectives on crime causation, criminal justice administration and crime prevention* (pp. 33-52). Boston: Butterworth-Heinemann.

Taylor, J., & Grundy, C. (1996). Measuring black internalization of White stereotypes about African Americans: The Nadanolitization scale. In R. L. Jones (Ed.), *The handbook of tests and measurements for black populations* (pp. 217-226). Oakland, CA: Cobb & Henry.

Taylor, J., & Turner, R. J. (2002). Perceived discrimination, social stress, and depression in the transition to adulthood: Racial contrasts. *SOCIAL PSYCHOLOGY QUARTERLY, 65,* 213-225.

Terrell, F., & Terrell, S. L. (1981). An inventory to measure cultural mistrust among Blacks. *Western Journal of Black Studies, 5,* 180-184.

Terrell, F., Terrell, S. L., & Miller, F. (1993). Level of cultural mistrust as a function of educational and occupational expectations among Black students. *Adolescence*, *28*, 573-578.

Terrell, F., Terrell, S. L., & Taylor, J. (1981). Effects of race of examiner and cultural mistrust on the WAIS performance of Black students. *Journal of Consulting and Clinical Psychology*, *49*, 750-751.

Thernstrom, A., & Thernstrom, S. (2003). In A. Thernstrom & S. Thernstrom (Eds.), *No excuses: Closing the racial gap in learning* (pp. 120-147). New York, NY: Simon & Schuster.

Thompson, C. E., & Neville, H. A. (1999). Racism, mental health, and mental health practice. *The Counseling Psychologist, 27,* 155–223.

Thompson, C. E., Neville, H., Weathers, P. L., Poston, W. C., & Atkinson, D. R. (1990). Cultural mistrust and racism reaction among African-American students. *Journal of College Student Development, 31,* 162-168.

Thompson, V. L. (2002). Racism: Perceptions of distress among African Americans. *Community Mental Health Journal, 38,* 111–118.

Tinsley-Jones, H. (2001). Racism: calling a spade a spade. *Psychotherapy: Theory, Research, Practice, Training, 40,* 179-186.

Tolan, P. H., Gorman-Smith, D., Henry, D., Chung, K., & Hunt, M. (2002). The relation of patterns of coping of inner-city youth to psychopathology symptoms. *Journal of Research on Adolescence, 12,* 423-449.

Tucker, C., Herman, K., Pedersen. T., Vogel, D., & Reinke, W. (2000). Student generated solutions to enhance the academic success of African-American youth. *Child Study Journal, 30,* 205-222.

Tucker, C. M., Zayco, R. A., & Herman, K. C. (2002). Teacher child variables as predictors of academic engagement among low-income African American children. *Psychology in the Schools, 39,* 477-488.

U.S. Census Bureau (1982). *Current population survey: Consumer income series.* Washington, DC: U.S. Department of Commerce.

U.S. Census Bureau. (1999). *Statistical abstract of the United States: 1999.* Washington, DC: U. S. Government Printing Office.

U.S. Census Bureau. (2000). *Profile of selected social characteristics: Allegany County, N.Y.* Retrieved January 25, 2010, from http://factfinder.census.gov/servlet/QTTable?_bm=y&-qr_name=DEC_2000_SF3_U_DP2&ds_name=DEC_2000_SF3_U&-_lang=en&-_sse=on&-geo_id=05000US36003

U.S. Department of Health and Human Services. (1999). *Mental health: A report of the Surgeon General.* Rockville, MD: Author.

U.S. Department of Health and Human Services. (2001). Mental health, culture, race and ethnicity. Rockville, MD: Author.

U.S. Department of Justice. (2007). *Fact sheet: Civil rights division efforts to combat modern-day slavery.* Retrieved March 2, 2009, from, http://www.usdoj.gov/opa/pr/2007/January/07_crt_061.html

Utsey, S. O. (1997). Racism and the psychological well-being of African American men. *Journal of African American Men, 3,* 69–87.

Utsey, S. O. (1999). Development and validation of a short form of the Index of Race-Related Stress (IRRS)–Brief version. *Measurement and Evaluation in Counseling and Development, 32,* 149-167.

Utsey, S. O., & Ponterotto, J. G. (1996). Development and validation of the Index of Race-Related Stress (IRRS). *Journal of Counseling Psychology, 43*, 490-502.

Wahl, O. F. (1999). *Telling is risky business—Mental health consumers confront stigma.* New Brunswick, NJ: Rutgers University Press.

Wellman, D. (1977). *Portraits of White racism.* Berkeley, CA: University of California Press.

White, J. L., & Parham, T. A. (1990). *The psychology of Blacks: An African-American perspective.* Englewood Cliffs, NJ: Prentice-Hall.

Williams, D. R., Neighbors, H. W., & Jackson, J. S. (2003). Racial/ethnic discrimination and health: Findings from community studies. *American Journal of Public Health, 93,* 200-208.

Williams, D. R., & Williams-Morris, R. (2000). Racism and mental health: The African American experience. *Ethnicity & Health, 5,* 243–268.

Williams, D. R., Yu, Y., Jackson, J. S., & Anderson, N. B. (1997). Racial differences in physical and mental health: Socioeconomic status, stress and discrimination. *Journal of Health Psychology, 2,* 335-351.

Wilson, D., Warton, C., & Louw, G. (1998). Stress, anxiety and academic performance among medical students in the University of Cape Town. *Southern African Journal of Child and Adolescent Mental Health, 10,* 23-31.

Wolchik, S. A., & Sandler, I. N. (Eds.). (1997). *Handbook of children's coping with common life stressors: Linking theory, research and interventions.* New York: Plenum.

Made in the USA
Monee, IL
12 November 2026

68342122R00125